Secrets To A Blissful ~~~~~~~~~~y &
Painfree Childbirth

Veronica Anusionwu

The Lord's Word On Healing Series

The Lord's Word On Healing Publications

The *BMA Family Health Encyclopedia* (Dorling Kindersley).

Unless otherwise indicated, bible quotes are from the *New International Version,* © 1973, 1978, 1984 by the International Bible Society, and used by kind permission of Hodder & Stoughton. Other editions quoted from include *The Amplified Bible, Old Testament,* © 1965, 1987 by the Zondervan Corporation; *The Amplified New Testament* © 1958, 1987 by the Lockman Foundation, used with kind permission, and *The King James Version of The Bible.*

ISBN 0-9532698-7-6

Printed in England

TABLE OF CONTENTS

A<small>UTHOR</small>'s P<small>REFACE</small>

LET'S GET RID OF THE OLD WIVES TALES

For thousands of years, all kinds of negative talk, negative views, and ideas have been presented about pregnancy. Old wives tales abound of how difficult and painful it is for women to have children. Any sight of frustration or anger is equated with the behaviour of a pregnant woman.

The idea of painful childbirth has been glamorised by the TV industry; everyday our children watch childbirth on TV dramatised as a thing of woe and pain. No wonder they grow up believing that childbirth will be painful for them.

In the churches ministers use painful childbirth experiences in their sermons, no wonder than that we all have grown up hearing and believing that childbirth will be painful as this portrays an idea that God wants the woman to suffer in childbirth. Yet a careful study of the bible teaches us that painful childbirth is a curse. Each time the Bible talks about painful childbirth it is equated to a curse. Let's take three scriptural examples:

> Wail for the day of the Lord is near; it will come like destruction from the Almighty. Because of this all hands will go limp, every man's heart will melt. Terror will seize them, pain and anguish will grip them; they will writhe like a **woman in labour**. They will look aghast at each other, their faces aflame, (Isaiah 13:6-8).

> When you disciplined them, they could barley whisper a prayer. As a **woman with child** and about to give birth writhes and cries out in her pain, so were we in your presence, O Lord. We were with child, we writhed in pain, but we gave birth to wind, (Isaiah 26:16-18).

Why do you now cry aloud-have you no king? Has your counsellor perished that pain seizes you like that of a **woman in labour**? Writhe in agony, O daughter of Zion, like a woman in **labour**, for now you must leave the city to camp in the open field. You will go to Babylon; there you will be rescued. There the Lord will redeem you out of the hand of your enemies, (Micah 4:9-10).

What can we do? How do we start changing the negative ideas and beliefs we have about painful childbirth to positive so that men and women will change their views and ideas about pregnancy and childbirth? The first step is individual education. Each individual needs to renew their mind to know and understand that God never intended childbirth to be a painful experience but rather a blessing. This are just some of God's promises of easy childbirth:

- "No sooner is Zion in labour, then she gives birth to her children,"(Isaiah 66: 8).

- "Before Zion travailed, she gave birth; before her labour pain came upon her, she was delivered of a male child," (Isaiah 66: 7).

- "The Hebrew women are not like the Egyptian women, they are quickly delivered, and their babies are born before the midwife comes to them,"(Exodus 1: 19).

You can see that the greatest desire of God's heart is that all go well for us, even in pregnancy and childbirth. God wants every woman to know that her portion from him is blissful pregnancy and pain-free childbirth.

A tribute to mothers.

I praise the Father for His love and I thank Him for the privilege of giving this powerful truth to his beautiful daughters. Receive the blessing freely given to you and enjoy it. I want to pay this special tribute to mothers all over the world.

Tribute

My dear sister, I bless God for your life. God's desire for you is blissful pregnancy. Blissful pregnancy! What is blissful? The dictionary says blissful is complete happiness, paradise, and heaven. God created you as a woman to glorify him. You carry the Seed of the woman, Seed blessed by God. Pregnancy was ordained by God to be a time of happiness and physical stability for you. A heavenly experience. Unbearable pain, sickness and disease in pregnancy and childbirth are not your portion from the Lord. God created you to excel in everything you do even in pregnancy and child bearing; you are fearfully and wonderfully made and equipped for this assignment by your Lord. You are a mighty woman in the hand of God. You are a co -labourer with your Lord. You are a life giver. You are precious to your Lord and He says to you "my daughter I love you". "I want your pregnancy to be a heavenly and paradise experience, as you receive my word, you will never suffer again in pregnancy or childbirth. Now taste and see that I am good".

Introduction

Childbirth is one of the primary factors in life. It is essential to the survival of the human race and it is the first commandment given by God to man, (Genesis: 3:26).

The mention of the word motherhood creates an atmosphere of reverence. Men, consciously and subconsciously, react with all the male instincts of preservation and protection when in its presence. A woman with child or her child is beyond the law of conflict. Injury to mothers and their young is considered the worst form of cruelty. Tenderness is an emotion primarily designed by nature to protect the defenceless. It is an emotion mainly experienced by men when in the presence of women. A woman herself starts from childhood to prepare herself for this great role of motherhood. From childhood she is busy bathing her doll, dressing it up, feeding it and caring for it.

All that is most beautiful in her life is associated with the emotions leading up to this ultimate function. There is no other joy that can compare to the joy of meeting someone, "falling in love" getting engaged and getting married. The average woman associates all that is beautiful in her life with these series of events. Unfortunately, in the final perfection of these joy, a large number of women remember only the pain and anguish and even terror that they are called upon to endure at the birth of their first child.

This to me is a paradox; we must ask this question and allow the Holy Spirit to answer it for us. Does God lead women along the course of essential purpose by bringing her into contact with irresistible demands of all that is beautiful? Is she led on from one joy to another by some force which intends to make her pay eventually the price by pain before she can achieve her dreams of holding her child in her arms? If this is keeping with the law of nature what can its purpose be?

For generations childbirth has been accepted as a dangerous and painful experience. Is a woman expected to arrive at her perfection by the exhibition of beauty on the one hand and suffering on the other? In blissful pregnancy and painfree childbirth, I bring you truth from the living Word of God to teach you that you can have your pregnancy and baby without sorrow. It is time for us to raise pregnancy and childbirth to its rightful position in Christ Jesus. It is supposed to be a heavenly experience. This book is written to help destroy some of the lies of the enemy concerning this glorious calling "pregnancy and childbirth". God bless you as you read.

Veronica Anusionwu

Chapter 1

The History of Childbirth

In this chapter I will like to share briefly with you certain facts relating to childbirth during the later stages of civilisation. The human race has existed for thousands of years and yet as I read many old books I discovered that the pain of childbirth always has been the heritage of woman because nothing in our modern teaching has enabled us to prevent it. It is believed, because it has always existed.

In our days a lot of scientific discoveries have been made to help ease the pain of childbirth. The more the civilisation of a country the more generally pain has been accepted as a symptom of childbirth. Even with all the medical pain relief available pain is accepted as part of childbirth. It is so acceptable that recently a friend went into hospital to deliver her baby. The baby was ready to be born and the midwife told her to take a sit. She was telling the midwife she felt like pushing but the midwife said to her "you can't feel like pushing you just got here". The midwife's assistants said to her "just go and examine the lady" When she did she discovered that the baby was almost out. They now went into a quick delivery to get the baby out. Most doctors and midwives do not believe that a woman can deliver her child without labour pains.

Many old writings suggest that herbs and portion were used to relieve women in labour. Witchcraft was resorted to very successfully. Three thousand years before Christ, the priest among the Egyptians were called to women in labour. In fact it may be said with some accuracy that amongst the most primitive people of which any record exists, help according to the customs of the time was given to women in labour. In Genesis 3:16 we read of where God said to Eve "I will greatly multiply thy sorrow and thy conception; in sorrow thou shall bring forth children." This particularly verse of scripture has been abused over the years where by many have believed that a woman, because of her sin was condemned to a multitude of sorrow and pain, particularly in the conception, bearing and bringing up of her child. This had considerable influence among Christian communities in ancient times.

Even as late as the middle of the nineteenth century this was quoted by clerical and medical authorities as justification for opposition to any active relief of the sufferings of women in labour. In 1884 Simpson first used anaesthesia. On April 7th 1853, John Snow anaesthized Queen Victoria when prince Leopold was born. For the use of anaesthetics for this purpose, Simpson was harshly criticised by the church. To prevent pain during childbirth he was told was contrary to religion and the express command of scriptures. He had no right "to rob God of the deep, earnest cries" of women in labour.

But anaesthetic had come to stay. A year later Florence Nightingale was the first woman to make it widely known that cleanliness and fresh air were fundamental necessities of nursing. It was largely because of her work during the Crimean war that the standard of both the training and the practice of nursing were raised. The gin-drinking reprobates who were found in great numbers among midwives began to disappear. With their exodus, childbirth fever occurred less frequently in midwives cases.

In a maternity hospital in Vienna, medical student's cases showed an average over a period of six years of ninety-nine deaths per thousand from puerperal fever. Semmelweis, who was physician at the hospital at the time (1858) believed the cause to be due to something arising within the hospital, and made his students, wash their hands in a solution of chloride of lime. In one year the death rate in his ward went from 18 to 3 per cent and then to 1 percent. This success necessitated his facing opposition and hostility from those around him. But his work was done; he laid a foundation stone of safer childbirth.

In 1866, Dr Lister brought us the knowledge of antiseptics, which he continued to employ in spite of the opposition and ridicule of his colleagues. Gradually, truth has been discovered, the safety of women has been the object of investigation with results that that would have been unbelievable when the great grand mother and our grand mothers were born.

Over the years many of the dangers of childbirth has been overcome. We must now move on, not only to save more lives, but also actually bring happiness to replace the agony of pain and fear. We must bring a fuller life to women who are called upon by God to bear children and replenish the earth. The joy of a new life, must be the vision of motherhood, instead of the fear of pain that has clouded it since civilisation developed.

Today I give the Lord all the glory for allowing me to write a book like this. I pray that any man or woman who will read this book will receive a renewed mind as to how they view pregnancy and childbirth. I pray for pregnant women all over the world that a blissful pregnancy and painfree childbirth will be their testimony as they read and apply the truth in this book. I pray that your pregnancy will be comfortable, full of joy and glory in the name of Jesus. I pray that the noble task of motherhood will be fulfilling for every woman who reads this book. God bless you.

Chapter 2

The Role of the Holy Spirit In Your Life during your pregnancy and delivery

In this chapter, I will like to introduce you to the Holy Spirit, the person who wrote this book so that the blessing of God may come into your life. Before I go any further, I would like to tell you this; 'Jesus loves you and cares about you.' He has created you as a woman to bring forth children and you are precious to your Lord.

Do you know the Holy Spirit? If your answer is no, allow me the privilege to introduce Him to you. He is the One who wrote this book, to the glory of Jesus Christ, so that the blessings and goodness of God will come to you. He is the One Whom Jesus left on earth for us. For the Lord Jesus Christ, before He left to go back to the Father, promised us this:

"I will ask the Father and He will give you another Counselor to be with you forever, the Spirit of truth. The world cannot accept Him because they neither see Him nor know Him. But you know Him, for He lives with you and will be in you. I will not leave you as orphans. I will come to you, (John 14:16-18).

From this passage you can see that the Holy Spirit is already here on earth with us. But it is strange to have Him with us and yet totally miss His presence and His love, because we do not even know He is with us. You say, I call Him '**He?** Yes, the Holy Spirit of God is a person. He is not a mere influence or power coming from God. He is a real person. Jesus said, *"that He may abide with you."* He is here to help us and teach us all things if we will allow Him. I desire that you as an expectant mother know Him for yourself because He is the person who will help you to reap all the blessings in this book.

The Holy Spirit of God is here to help you to succeed in all you undertake to do including pregnancy and delivery. I want us to look into three different areas that I believe will be of benefit to you as you journey with the Lord during your blissful pregnancy and pain free childbirth. The Bible says *"that He may abide with you"*. The Holy Spirit is already here and is abiding with you.

The working of God the Father, God the Son, God the Holy Spirit is the mystery of the Gospel of Jesus Christ. It is better to accept it than to try to figure it out, for only in heaven will we clearly understand it all. Take what you have and apply it and let it work for you.

The Holy Spirit Quickens
The Bible says, "if the Spirit of God who raised Jesus from the dead is living in you, He will also quicken your mortal body" (Romans 8:11). What is to quicken? It means to make faster, to accelerate, to give or restore life or animation, to stimulate, to rouse, to inspire, to kindle, to cheer, to refresh, to move with increased rapidity, to receive life and vigour, to come to life.

Now we will break down the word **quicken** to help you see, know, understand and reap the full benefit of the quickening power of the Holy Spirit during your pregnancy and delivery.

The Holy Spirit makes things happen fast- to make happen faster means something happening quickly or with great speed. Swiftly and quickly accomplished. In rapid succession.

The Holy Spirit accelerates -What does it means to accelerate? It means to bring about an event at an earlier time. To increase the speed of. To hasten the progress, development or growth of. To move fast or faster. To gain speed. To increase. To move rapidly. To fix firmly or attached. Moving or able to move rapidly. Taking a comparatively short time. Quick to learn. Quickly or in quick succession.

The Holy Spirit stimulates- to stimulate means to excite you to greater activity by making your body work faster increasing your heart rate. If something stimulates you it gives you new ideas and enthusiasm. To arouse or affect by the action of a stimulant to encourage to begin or develop. To act as a stimulant or stimulus something that causes a process or event to begin or develop.

The Holy Spirit rouses - that is He makes you feel very emotional and excited. He can rouse you by making you face up to things.

The Holy Spirit can inspire- that is by giving you new ideas and enthusiasm to do something. To inspire an emotion in someone is to make him or her feel this emotion.

The Holy Spirit can kindle- if you kindle a fire you light it. If something kindles a feeling in you it causes you to have that feeling.

The Holy Spirit animates – to animate means to make it lively and interesting. To give it life. To rouse or cause to become aroused. To stir up or provoke. To rouse one from sleep or apathy. To inspire, to inhale. He can influence or guide you by divine inspiration. To breathe in, to blow or breathe upon.

The Holy Spirit can cheer you up - that is He can instil you with hope or courage, He can comfort you or make you glad or happy, remember He is the Comforter. He can urge you on or encourage you especially by shouts of approval. He aids growth and brings cheerfulness in every situation. If your environment is gloomy you can ask him to brighten it up and make it pleasant. He helps us to rejoice by filling us with His peace and joy.

The Holy Spirit refreshes – when something refreshes you when you are hot or tired, it makes you feel cooler or more energetic. Which means He can restore strength and vigour to you. He can revive you by using good food and rest. He can and will maintain you and restore you by renewing your supplies supernaturally. He can also replenish you. The Holy Spirit is truly the one who refreshes.

The Holy Spirit gives vigour- when you have vigour, you have active strength. You do things with vigour, carried out forcefully and energetically. You are active physically and mentally and full of strength. You flourish. It is also well balanced healthy growth especially of plants.

The Holy Spirit's quickening power

The Holy Spirit's quickening power is the only power on earth that can fasten your delivery and make it pain free. During your pregnancy He will inspire and kindle His goodness in you. During your delivery, He will quicken and accelerate your contractions. He will hasten its progress. Where those who don't know Him are in labour for hours on end He will hasten everything and bring it to a swift finish for you. He will cheer you up in the delivery room; after all He is our Cheerleader and Comforter. After delivery He will refresh you and rekindle the fire of God in you. In the Holy Spirit's quickening power is everything needed for a blissful pregnancy and painfree childbirth.

The benefit of His quickening power

Remember we said to accelerate means to increase the speed or rate of progress, or to hasten or bring nearer in point of time. T increase in velocity, to move faster or the ability to gain spe rapidly. I just want to encourage my sisters, who are exp baby, the bible actually tells us that the Holy Spirit can make your pregnancy and labour and childbirth pain-free.

Whatever you need or require He is able to do for you. Everything you need for a blissful pregnancy and painfree childbirth has already been given to you. It is now time to enjoy all the benefits freely given to us by our heavenly Father as we receive with thanksgiving all that Christ has accomplished for us.

In the following chapters we will be using the quickening power of the Holy Spirit to enforce the Word of God in all areas of pregnancy. Please remember in this pregnancy you are not alone but you are working together with the Holy Spirit to reap all the best He has already provided for you in your pregnancy.

The Holy Spirit Strengthens

The Spirit of the Living God is the one that gives strength, for the Bible says when we are weak, He is strong. He can give strength in any area of our life that requires strength. To strengthen means to make strong or stronger, to increase in strength, to empower some-one to take action. The Holy Spirit is the one who gives strength. The Holy Spirit supplies support and power in your life. He is the one that can make you strong in all areas of your life.

The Bible says, we can do all things through Christ who gives us strength, (Phillpians 4:13). You can have your baby without hassles because the Spirit of God gives you strength to do all things. The ause of faith Sarah herself received physical power ld, even when she was long past the age for l). Yes! Sarah received strength from the Holy t a very old age and to have a blissful pregnancy, red God faithful. This is the kind of specialist es. You also can receive strength from Him to cy and pain-free childbirth. Why not? The o more than we can ever ask or imagine s 3: 20. For the pregnant woman the Word of

God guarantees you strength in all your endeavors including having children. Let us look at some of these promises of strength.

- The Lord is my strength and my shield; my heart trusts in Him, and I am helped. My heart leaps for joy and I will give thanks to Him in song.
- The Lord is the strength of my life; of whom shall I be afraid? (Psalm 27:1).
- The Lord gives strength to His people; the Lord blesses His people with peace, (Psalm 29:11).
- The salvation of the righteous is from the Lord, He is their strength in the time of trouble (Psalm: 37:39).

After the birth of your baby, you need to know him as the one who renews

Every woman who has gone through nine months of pregnancy knows what she needs. She needs rest and to be renewed. The Spirit of the Living God is the one who renews life. What does it mean to renew? It means to make new again or as good as new, to renovate, to make fresh or vigorous again. To reanimate, to revivify, to regenerate, to replace something old or worn out with new. To replenish, to get, make, say etc. To grant or be given a further period of validity or effectiveness. Wow! What a promise! The Word of God says the Holy Spirit can renew you.

He will renew you and help you regain your health and beauty after your pregnancy and delivery. He will make you look fresh and young and vigorous again, He will reanimate you. He will encourage you, give you a new spirit and a fresh start. The Spirit of God will truly make you appear young again. He will reactivate you and bring you back in vogue and vigour. He will replenish you and fill you up again with new energy. The Holy Spirit of the Living God is truly the one who renews. The One who can help you to renew your mind concerning all the negative ideas you have believed about pregnancy and childbirth.

Now pray the Holy Spirit will help you to renew your mind with the living Word of God.

Prayer

Holy Spirit I worship you. Father I bless you, in the mighty name of Jesus, I choose to put off all the negative talk or ideas I have about pregnancy and childbirth. I put off my old self and I choose to be made new in the attitude of my mind; and to put on the new self, created to be like God in true righteousness and holiness, (Ephesians 4:22). I chose to abandon all the negative ideas I have about pregnancy and I embrace the truth that comes from you. Holy Spirit I thank you because I know you have helped me in the name of Jesus.

Create in me O Lord a clean heart, and renew a steadfast spirit within me, (Psalm 51:10). I put on the new man who is renewed in knowledge according to the image of Him who created me, (Colossians 3:10). By the help of the Holy Spirit I refuse to conform any longer to the pattern and belief of this world system in regards to childbirth and pregnancy, but I am transformed by the renewing of my mind and I embrace the truth from the Word of God. I am able to test and approve what God's will is, His good and pleasing and perfect will concerning my pregnancy and childbirth, (Romans12: 2). I declare according to the Word of God that the Lord has perfected everything concerning me. The Lord who has started His good work of creation in me will complete it, (Phillipians 1:6). God's will for my baby and me is to prosper and be in good health. God is at work in me now to will and do His good pleasure. The power of the Holy Spirit is at work in me right now. It is flowing in me and perfecting all that which pertains to my baby's formation in Jesus name.

Holy Spirit I thank you because I know you will help me and see me through in the mighty name of Jesus. Amen.

Chapter 3

What is childbirth? Medical background

Childbirth is the process by which a baby moves out of its mothers womb into the out side world. After 38 or 40 weeks of pregnancy, which is normally from the time, the woman had her last menstrual period.

In developed countries of the world, because of proper antenatal care childbirth presents no serious problems. In developing countries where antenatal care is poor women die during childbirth more than in developed countries of the world.

In the past few years women have become concerned because of the over mechanization of the issue of childbirth in most hospitals which has now led to the popularity of "natural child birth" which does not encourage the use of unnecessary medical intervention. Many hospitals now recognise that women have the right to choose the type of birth they would like as far as those choices do not in any way endanger the life of the mother or baby. Choice of pain relief, position of the birth is now left to the woman.

Signs of labour

It is not always easy to tell when labour has started. But the following signs may be helpful, contractions that becomes progressively more painful at regular or shorter intervals.

A show which is a bloody discharge of the mucus plug that has blocked the cervical canal during pregnancy. Breaking of the waters. This may vary from one woman to the other it could gush out suddenly in some, and in others it could be a tickle of fluid from the vagina.

There are three stages of labour.

Stage 1 – the beginning of labour to the time when the cervix is fully dilated.
Stage 2 – from fully dilated cervix to delivery of the baby.
Stage 3 – delivery of baby to the expulsion of the placenta, which is also, called the "after birth".

Chapter 4

Pain relief

These are the various medical pain relief's available to help women cope with pain during labour.

Epidural- an anaesthetic that helps relives pain by temporary numbing the nerves in the lower body. Some women feel faint and have a headache and some have heavy legs after an Epidural.

Entonox (Gas & air) A mixture of oxygen and nitrous oxide, which relives pain by making you, feel euphoric.

Pethidine-

Often given during the early stages of labour, especially where a woman is anxious or unable to relax.

Tens

This is a machine that lessens pain and stimulates the body's natural system of pain relief through small impulses of electric currents on your back. Some women say it offers no help at all if their labour is painful.

Gas

This takes the edge off the pain, which may not be enough. Effects- a light headed or sick feeling.

Peth

Some women feel calm, relaxed and a bit sleepy- others complain of being out of control or feeling drunk, sick and tiredness.

Chapter 5

Special procedures

Some of these procedures are used by the medical professional to assist women during delivery or labour.

Episiotomy: this is where a small cut is done to widen the vagina opening and prevent a tear.
Vacuum: A small metal cap connected to a vacuum pump. This will be passed into the vagina and attached to the baby's head. The baby will then be gently pulled through the birth canal, as you push.
Induction: This is where labour is started artificially. It could be used to speed up labour if it is going slow.
Breaking your water: Here the doctor makes a small hole in the bag of water surrounding the baby.
Giving you a hormone: This makes the womb contract.

Confession
Father I bless you because you are faithful to complete what you started in my life. I Command in the name of Jesus that my pelvic floor relax. I reject premature birth, breech baby, distressed baby or any form of difficulty in pregnancy and childbirth. The quickening power of the Holy Spirit is upon me, by His power my vagina walls will stretch perfectly to allow my baby's head to pass blissfully through my birth canal.

I will not need the medical professionals to get my baby out with forceps or by suction. I thank you Father that the quickening power of the Holy Spirit that is within me stimulates my womb for a quick and swift delivery. I ask that you guide my pregnancy and take full control of my life. The power of the Holy Spirit knows when to break my water and when it is time He will animate my water and it will break normally. My contractions will be normal because His power has accelerated it and made it painfree, it will be regular and I will dilate perfectly.

My baby will not die in my womb. My womb will enlarge in the way ordained by God to accommodate my baby. My baby will come out on its due date alive and well in the name of Jesus, Jeremiah: 2017. I declare that every disease and germ should die now in Jesus name. Nothing I take into my body through the mouth shall harm me according to, Mark 16: 18.

I reject any false starts like braxton hick's contractions. As I walk into the hospital my doctor and midwife will be ready and waiting to deliver me swiftly. My cervix will be gradually softened by the quickening power of the Holy Spirit. The contractions will be normal; the stretching will be perfect and just normal to allow my baby's head to pass through my birth canal. I reject backache in labour.

I decree in this pregnancy that "My baby's head move swiftly through my vaginal opening, my baby's head moves forward". The head of my baby is born face down just like Rebekah had her twins. My cervix will be fully dilated and as I push, my baby will be born without any pain to me. Just one push and every thing will be over.

The umbilical cord comes out on it's own. The cord will not slip over my baby's neck. My baby will not swallow the amniotic fluid. My baby's breath will be normal. I will hear my baby's cry for the first time. The placenta will follow immediately, It will come out completely and nothing will be left in my womb. The umbilical cord is perfect. I reject any form of tear or bleeding disorder.

I praise you Lord, as they clean me up and I walk to the rest ward with my baby I will continue to praise you. I bless you Lord Jesus because you have glorified your name in my life and shown me that truly, blissful pregnancy and painfree childbirth is my heritage from you and is possible by the quickening power of the Holy Spirit.

Reject all discomfort and after delivery pains

After delivery pains! I reject you in the name of Jesus. Any felling of cramping pain in the stomach, especially when I breast feed my baby, you are not part of this pregnancy and delivery. My stomach will contract back to normal in Jesus name. My bladder will return back to normal. I will not experience any problem when I urinate. I reject abnormal bleeding after delivery. My bowls will move perfectly as I eat well-balanced and healthy food and drink a lot of fluid. I reject any infection after delivery. I give thanks and praise to you Father in Jesus name. Amen.

Chapter 6

Pain is not part of the Covenant

Over the years, man has developed various methods to help women overcome labour pains. In spite of all these developments the fear of labour pain is still real in the life of millions of women all over the world. If we studied the bible carefully, we will discover that the kind of pain dramatised on TV which is what our children watch and which also help shape their mental attitude is a lie. That childbirth must be accompanied with pain is false.

God actually ordained childbirth to be blissful and wonderful for every woman. In **Genesis**, God said "unto the woman, I will greatly multiply thy **sorrow**; and thy conception, in sorrow shall thou bring forth children,"(Genesis 3:16). God pronounced the curse of pain in childbirth on the woman because of sin and disobedience. Before the disobedience of Adam and Eve there was nothing like pain in childbirth. But we have the good news of deliverance from the curse of sorrow in the death and resurrection of Jesus Christ. After the curse of sorrow was pronounced on the woman, (Isaiah 53: 4-5) tells us Christ came and redeemed us from God's pronouncements. For the Bible declares "Christ took up all our infirmities and carried our **sorrows**, the punishment that brought us peace was upon him and by His wounds we are healed". Christ has redeemed every woman from the curse and sorrow of painful childbirth by becoming a curse for her "for it is written, cursed is anyone that is hung on a tree". He redeemed us in order that the blessings given to Abraham might come to us Gentiles through Jesus Christ," (Galatians 3: 13-14). "He himself bore all our sins in His body on the tree, so that we might die to sin and live for righteousness, by His wounds you have been healed,"(1 Peter 2:24). Healed from problem pregnancy and painful labour.

In the mouth of two or three witnesses a truth is confirmed. Christ has already paid the price and borne the pain of painful childbirth on the cross for every woman who chooses to believe and receive it. He carried the punishment that brought us peace. Yes! He paid the price in all things including childbirth. He himself carried the *sorrow* that was multiplied to the woman in Genesis. In Isaiah 53:4 He paid the price so that you can have your baby without sorrow. Why is it that even though Christ has paid the full price we are still having pain and sorrow during childbirth? The first answer is our mindset. From childhood all we hear is how painful childbirth is. A little girl grows up believing in her mind that childbirth will be a painful experience for her; because that's what she's heard and seen on TV all her life.

The second reason is ignorance of the Word of God. Many women are ignorant of what God has for them in the area of childbirth. Pain in childbirth is not the will of God for you and me, sister; it is not our inheritance from God, it is His desire that you walk into the delivery ward and walk out with your baby without having suffered hardship and pain. That is the reason why Christ bore the sorrow on the cross for you and me so that we don't have to bear it.

Let us look at some biblical promise from our Father concerning pain-free childbirth

- "No sooner is Zion in labour, then she gives birth to her children,"(Isaiah 66: 8).
- "Before Zion travailed, she gave birth; before her labour pain came upon her, she was delivered of a male child," (Isaiah 66: 7).
- "The Hebrew women are not like the Egyptian women, they are quickly delivered, and their babies are born before the midwife comes to them"(Exodus 1: 19).
- "The Bible says to the woman "breakforth and cry aloud, you who have no labour pains", (Isaiah 54:1).

Mary the mother of Jesus is a testimony in the bible of a woman who gave birth on her own, she did not have help and yet she brought her baby forth on her own. Galatians 4:27 says, "those under the promise and the blessings of God, those who walk in faith knowing that God loves them and truly cares for them; are the ones that have no labour pains". As you go into these meditation confessions bear this truth in mind, Isaiah 53: 4-6, already solves the pain issue for us "he himself bore all your sickness and pain on the cross by whose stripes you were healed". Christ bore your pain on the cross. The price of painful childbirth was paid for you on the cross of Cavalry. Christ took that pain and you don't have to suffer in pregnancy. Now sisters make your declaration of victory over pain in childbirth.

Confession

The Father has assigned me my portion and my cup; He has made my pregnancy secure. The boundary lines have fallen for me in pleasant places; surely I have a delightful inheritance. Christ bore the pain and sorrow of childbirth for me; I do not have to bear it anymore. The punishment that brought me peace was laid on Christ, so peace in pregnancy and childbirth is my portion. I refuse to partake of the curse of painful childbirth. I am a child of God, I belong to the family of those who "before they travail, give birth; before their labour pain comes upon them are already delivered of their child," (Isaiah 66: 7). Blissful pregnancy and pain- free childbirth is my portion and heritage in Jesus name.

"The blessing of the Lord makes one rich and adds no sorrow with it, (Proverbs 10:27). Children are a heritage from the Lord, and He adds no sorrow to His blessing. I refuse to experience sorrow in this pregnancy or during childbirth, because the blessings of the Lord add no sorrow. Because of what this verse of scripture says I believe that I am delivered from the curse of sorrow in childbirth.

I am like "The Hebrew women, I am not like the Egyptian women, I am quickly delivered, of my baby even before the midwife comes to me,"(Exodus 1:19). Because of the quickening power of the Holy Spirit. I am a strong and vigorous woman; I am quickly delivered of my baby, like the great women of old who trusted in God, I do not suffer any labour pains. I choose to enjoy a blissful pregnancy and go on to have a pain-free childbirth. Thank you Father in Jesus name. Amen.

Chapter 7

Let's deal with the fear of labour pains

For years women have lived with the dreaded fear of problems in pregnancy and labour pain. You will be amazed to discover the amount of fear that goes through the mind of a pregnant woman. A woman came to me recently who told me she couldn't wait for this book to come out. She said to me "Veronica I always have problems from the beginning to the end of my pregnancy". Many women experience pain from the beginning to the end of their pregnancy and this is in contradiction to the Word of God for the woman.

What is fear? It is an emotion, which arises from the primary instinct of fright. It is alertness to the presence of danger; it is the natural protective agent, which enables the individual to escape from danger. What danger is the pregnant woman running from that makes her so afraid during her pregnancy? The Bible warns us about fear. God is not the author of fear. Anything that brings fear is not of God. How can something as beautiful as childbirth become a fearful experience? Yet this is the experience of millions of women all over the world. The Bible says, "God has not given us the spirit of fear, but the spirit of power, love and a sound mind". Fear does not come from God. God is a God of faith. Today I want you to listen to what God has to say to us in His Word about fear.

- "Fear not, I will nourish you and your little ones,"(Genesis 50: 21).
- "Peace! Do not be afraid. You are not going to die,"(Judges 6:21).

- "Fear not, I am the first and the last,"(Revelation 1: 17).
- "Say to those with fearful hearts, "be strong, do not fear; your God will come," (Isaiah 35:4).
- "The angel said to the woman, do not be afraid," (Matthew 28:5).

The Lord Jesus Christ who is the first and the last says to you His daughter," do not be afraid". As you go into these confessions my beloved sister, I want you to hold your head up high, "do not be afraid for the Lord your God is with you, He will surely give you a blissful pregnancy and pain-free childbirth. For His perfect love in your life has cast out all fear. "I love you".

Confession

Now sisters make these confessions to get rid of fear throughout your pregnancy.

I am a child of God, a daughter of Sarah, I do what is right and I do not give way to fear, 1st Peter 3:16. I choose to trust the Lord who gave Sarah a blissful pregnancy and pain-free childbirth at 91 years, that He has done the same for me. I will not fear though the earth be removed, and the mountains fall into the heart of the sea, I refuse to allow the spirit of fear to come near me throughout this pregnancy, for I know that the Lord is my refuge and my strength, (Psalm 46:1-2). The Lord Almighty is with me, the God of Jacob is my fortress, and I am safe and secure in him. I have no need to fear what they fear or dread what they dread, for the Lord Almighty is the only one I am to fear. The Lord is my shield and my reward; I am safe from problem pregnancy and painful labour. He is my ever present help in every situation," (Genesis 15: 31).

The Father has made me a joyous mother of my child; my heart is fixed on the Lord. I refuse to be afraid. I will continue to thrive and blossom throughout this pregnancy like a tree planted in the courts of the Lord. Blissful pregnancy, pain-free delivery is my portion from the Lord and I choose to enjoy every moment of it. Thank you Father in Jesus' name- Amen.

Chapter 8

Common Complaints

In this chapter we are going to look at some of the common complaints that women experience during pregnancy. We will bring solution from the blissful Word of God that does not fail to help you avoid these common complaints and truly have a blissful pregnancy. Why not! This is God's perfect will for you. For the fruit of the womb is a reward from him and children are a heritage from Him. How can God reward you with pain and misery in your pregnancy. Take your stand now against these common complaints. Because the doctors say you are supposed to experience theses things does not mean you have to. Anything that contradicts the Word of God in your life, you have every right to reject in the name of Jesus. If Christ bore all your disease on the cross why do you have to bear it again? If you believe your God it is now time for you to speak His word. Lets take a look at the medical background of these complaints.

Bleeding gums -A pregnant woman could easily bleed from the gum especially after brushing her teeth. This is because the gum becomes softer and more easily injured during pregnancy. Inflammation could also occur, allowing plaque to collect at the base of the teeth. This could easily lead to gum disease.

Breathlessness -Feeling breathless when you exert yourself, or even when you walk. During the later part of pregnancy the growing baby puts pressure on the diaphragm, and this prevents a pregnant woman from breathing freely. Breathlessness can also be caused by anaemia.

Constipation -passing hard dry stools at less frequent intervals than usual.

Cramps -this is painful contraction of the muscles usually in the calves and the feet, and often at night. This may be as a result of calcium deficiency.

Eye changes- In pregnancy fluid retention also affects the shape of the eyeball. It's most noticeable in contact lens wearers, as the lens is designed to fit the shape of your eyeball

Feeling faint-Feeling dizzy and unstable. Needing to sit or lie down. Your blood pressure is lower in pregnancy so you are more likely to feel faint.

Frequent urination -A need to pass water more often. The uterus pressing on the bladder causes this.

Heartburn -A strong burning pain in the centre of the chest.

Leaking urine this is leakage of urine whenever you run, sneeze, laugh or cough caused by weak pelvic floor muscles and the growing baby pressing on your bladder.

Morning sickness- feeling sick, often at the smell of perfume, cigarettes or certain foods.

Oedema-If your face and arms get bigger, it probably because you are retaining fluid. Oedema, or water retention, is a common pregnancy complaint that is made worst by standing for long periods. The important thing to remember is that cutting down on fluid will not prevent oedema, but could in fact cause you and the baby harm. You should drink two litres of fluid everyday. Go easy on tea, coffee and cola because the caffeine will kill vitamins in your body, particularly vitamin c. after the birth of your baby, the way your body retains water will go back to normal.

Piles- Itching soreness and possible pain or bleeding when you pass stools.

Rash-This can be caused by hormone changes and can develop in sweaty skin folds, under the breast or in the groin.

Sleeping difficulty-There are many problems that can cause sleeping difficulty. The need to use the lavatory too often, the growing size of the baby makes you uncomfortable. Unpleasant dreams about the birth.

Painful wrists-This is a general swelling which occurs during pregnancy and can cause pressure on a nerve in the wrist which is known as carpal tunnel syndrome and can be quite painful. This condition usually goes away after the baby is born.

Nose bleed-Occasionally a pregnant woman could experience nosebleeds because of hormonal changes. This is usually short but can be quite heavy.

Stretch marks-These are red marks that sometimes appear on the stomach, skin and thighs or breast in pregnancy. The stretching of your skin during pregnancy causes stretch marks.

Sweating -This is caused by hormone changes and also because blood flow to the skin increases during pregnancy.

Swollen ankles and fingers-Slight swelling in the ankles or fingers.

Thrush-A thick white discharge and severe itching, it may also hurt and be a little sore when you pass water.

Tiredness-Feeling weary and wanting to sleep in the day. Need to sleep longer at night.

Vaginal discharge-Mostly due to hormone changes in the body during pregnancy.

Varicose veins- Aching legs, the veins in the calves and the thighs become painful and swollen

Bible confession for all areas of common complaint

My sister, now make your confession to overcome all areas of common complaints during your pregnancy. The power of life and death is in your tongue and your words have the power to set you free. The bible says by your word you will be justified and by your word you will be condemned, **Matthew 12:37**. Now use your word to justify yourself before God and man throughout your pregnancy.

<u>Now say it the way God says it</u>
Throughout my pregnancy I will walk in the light of the Lord and will not partake of the common problems that happen to women during pregnancy, (**Isaiah 2:5**). I am a woman of covenant and I have a covenant of peace with God. God has promised in His Word that it is well with me. That I will enjoy the fruit of my deeds, I choose to enjoy a blissful pregnancy and go ahead to have a pain-free delivery, (Isaiah 3:10). The glory of God is a canopy around me, my shelter and shade from the heat of all problems that occur in pregnancy.

The Lord is my refuge and my hiding place from the storm and rain, with the help of my Lord I sail victoriously through every problem that happen to women in pregnancy. Since problems in pregnancy is not part of the covenant that I have with the Lord. I choose to have a problem free pregnancy as I enjoy the best that the Father has for me, (Isaiah 4:5-6). I reject cramps, varicose veins, piles and backaches because Jesus Christ has borne all my sicknesses. I refuse constipation, anaemia, vitamin and mineral deficiencies, swollen hands and feet, hypertension, convulsion and diabetes in the mighty name of Jesus. My urine will remain normal in Jesus name (Psalm 103:3-5). I confess that the activities of eaters of flesh and drinkers of blood will not prosper in my life in Jesus name. I refuse and reject all negative dreams, visions, prophecies and imaginations in the name of Jesus.

Sleeping difficulty! You are not part of a blissful pregnancy and in the mighty name of Jesus I decree that throughout my pregnancy I will not grow weary or stumble, neither will I sleep unnecessarily, (Isaiah 5: 27) rather when I lie down to sleep my sleep will be sweet. I lie down and sleep in peace for the Lord makes me lie down in safety, (Psalms 4:8). God has already promised in His Word that when I run I will not grow weary, and when I walk l will not faint, I choose to believe the Word of God and I decree that this pregnancy will be blissful all the way, (Isaiah 40:31). Therefore tiredness during pregnancy is not my portion.

Bleeding gums! Throughout my pregnancy I will not suffer from bleeding gums, my teeth are perfect "like a flock of sheep coming up from the washing, each has it's twin, not one of them is alone,"(Song of Songs 6:6). The Lord is the strength of my life. My breath is perfect. My teeth are perfect.
My eyes! Are perfect. I have perfect eyes and pregnancy does not have to affect my eyesight.
Nosebleeds! I refuse to have **nosebleeds** in the name of Jesus. Thank you Father. Amen.

Constipation! *I* reject constipation in all its forms and I decree in the mighty name of Jesus that throughout this pregnancy my bowels will move perfectly. The quickening power of God *stimulates my bowel to move normally.* God helps me to eat wisely and wise eating enables my bowels to move Perfectly. Thank you Lord for good appetite to eat only healthy food in Jesus name. Thank you Father in the name of Jesus.

Cramps! Are not my portion and I reject it in the name of Jesus. Feeling dizzy and unstable is not part of the covenant and I refuse to feel faint and unstable during this pregnancy. In my pregnancy I have chosen to follow the way of God. Father I thank you for doing it for me in the same way as you did for all those women of faith who have walked and continue to walk with you in faith in the name of Jesus.

Urine! Praise God! My urine level is normal. I will pass urine in the normal way God ordained for it to be. Nothing abnormal whatsoever will affect my urine during this pregnancy.

Heartburn! Is far from me. Why should my heart burn? God is the strength of my heart. I reject heartburn; the Lord is the strength of my life.

Leaking urine! You are not my portion. Father, I thank you in the name of your Son Jesus Christ. My whole body joined and held together by every supporting ligament, grows and builds itself up in love, as each part does its work. My urine level remains perfect throughout this pregnancy. Thank you Lord, (Ephesians 4:16).

Morning sickness! You are not my lot. Reading through the pages of the bible I do not see any case of morning sickness. I know that this is not part of the covenant of peace that I have with the Lord. I refuse to partake of morning sickness. God said when I wake up from my sleep I will be refreshed. Morning sickness is not from the Lord; there is no where in the Word of God that I am promised morning sickness during pregnancy. The Word of God tells me that God's mercy will be renewed on me every morning and great is His faithfulness to me even in pregnancy and my delivery, (Lamentations 3:23). Therefore I reject morning sickness throughout this pregnancy. I confess that I am strong. Weakness is not my lot in Jesus name. I will not have morning sickness or vomiting in my pregnancy in Jesus name. I choose to enjoy a blissful pregnancy and go on to have a pain-free childbirth through the faithfulness of God. I also confess that I shall not suffer any sickness like nausea, irritation, headache, and internal or external pain because by the stripes of Jesus, I am healed. I thank you Father in Jesus name. Amen.

Painful wrists! I reject painful wrist in the name of Jesus. I shall enjoy the best that the Lord has for me in the name of Jesus. I will not suffer from pains in any part of my body because Christ has already borne my pains. Thank you father in Jesus name. Amen.

Oedema! Christ Jesus paid the price for me. I will not pay a second price for my joy and peace in pregnancy. My pregnancy is free from Oedema. The Holy Spirit of God is in full control of my pregnancy. His quickening power has made sure that my body fluid is normal. I praise you Lord because I know I will not suffer Oedema in my pregnancy. Thank you Lord.

Piles! You cannot come near, this pregnancy it is a blissful one. There is no room for piles and other irritating things that happen to women during pregnancy. I will pass my stool normally and there will be no blood or bleeding in the name of Jesus. My body is the temple of the Holy Spirit. I have the life and health of Christ in me. The sun of Righteousness has risen, having conquered sickness and pain and Satan. There is healing in His wings for me. No piles in Jesus name. Amen.

Rash! You are not part of the covenant of peace that I have with my Father during pregnancy. Even though my hormones may change during pregnancy it will not be accompanied by rash.

Stretch marks! You are not part of the deal and I reject you in the name of Jesus. You will not leave ugly scars on my tummy. I declare that in this pregnancy my skin will remain without any spot or blemish according to the Word of God in, (1st Samuel 14:25).

Sweating! You are not part of the covenant of peace that I have with the Lord. Hormone changes and blood flow to the skin will not make me sweat unnecessarily. I choose to have a perfect and blissful pregnancy and pain free childbirth.

Varicose Veins! Swollen ankles! Face! And fingers! You too you are not part of the covenant of peace that I have with the Lord. The children of God walked in the wilderness for forty-years and none of them had swollen legs and fingers. I refuse to accept swollen legs and fingers as part of this pregnancy, because this pregnancy is from the Lord, it is a heavenly one, (Deuteronomy 8:6)

Vaginal discharge! Thrush! You cannot come near me. My pregnancy is from the Lord. I have a covenant of peace in pregnancy with the Lord. Anything that will cause me vaginal discharges and itching is a disease and cannot be from the Lord. He already paid for all my disease according to Isaiah 53. I choose to have a pregnancy free from thrush and all irritations in the name of Jesus.

What a mighty God we serve! Father thank you for your love, you have chosen to teach me that I can have a blissful pregnancy and I choose to believe your word. I thank you Father in Jesus name. Amen.

Chapter 9

Breech baby and caesarean section

Breech birth – a breech baby is born bottom first. About 4 in 100 babies are breech. Labour with a breech baby can be difficult or longer than a normal positioned baby. Occasionally a caesarean is necessary.

Caesarean section – this is where the baby is delivered abnormally. These days some women choose to have a caesarean section and are given dates to come into hospital for this operation. In majority of cases it may be an emergency because of problems in labour.

You can use the confession from the Word of God, if you choose that you do not want to have a caesarean section. Pray the Word and start now. But if an emergency comes up you must listen to the professional advice of the doctors looking after you. Remember that because you have stood on the Word of God, He is in the doctors attending you and will also use them for your own good.

Engagement – this is the descent of the foetus head into its mothers pelvis. In most cases for a first pregnancy the foetus engages by 37 weeks, but in other pregnancies it may not engage till labour commences. The foetus may fail to engage if the baby is a breech or the head is too big for the mother's pelvic or where the placenta is in an abnormal position.

Fibroids- These are non-malignant growths in the uterus. Some times fibroids can occur in the womb and cause problem such as preventing the baby moving down into the pelvic ready to be born. Where this happens a caesarean section may be required. The fibroids are usually *r*emoved later in a separate operation.

Prayer

General Confession against having a breech baby and caesarean section

Listen to me my sister; we must act in wisdom. Using the Word of God, which cannot fail, always brings victory when we apply our faith, but you may find in some cases that your faith may not have developed enough to receive everything from God. If you are in labour and an emergency arises you must listen to the professional advice of the doctors and midwives attending to you. Our faith must never be turned to foolishness for our God uses doctors also and many lives are saved by the work of the doctors.

Now make your confession to help you over come having a breech baby or caesarean section.

Confession
Father I bless you because you are faithful to complete what you started in my life. You yourself said, you will not bring to the point of childbirth and not bring forth. Whatever you start you always complete and I bless you O Lord, because you are my help and my deliverer, and will not delay to deliver my baby for me safely, (Psalm 40:17).

I reject premature birth, breech baby, distressed baby or any form of difficulty in pregnancy and childbirth. My baby's head will pass swiftly through my birth canal. My baby is a child with wisdom, when the time arrives for delivery he or she will come to the opening of my womb, (Hosea 13: 13).

Caesarean section is not my portion. The spirit of the living God will stimulate and accelerate my delivery. I will have my baby in the normal way ordained by God. Father I bless you in the name of Jesus Christ because you are faithful. Lord in Genesis 25: 24-26, I saw how Rebekah gave birth to twins. Your Word tells me that "his brother came out with his hand grasping Esau's heel; so he was named Jacob," (Genesis 25: 24-26). From this scripture I can see clearly that the first one was upside down and the second one came out with his head down also which is the way ordained by you. I choose to have my baby come headfirst and I reject breech childbirth. The way you did it for Rebecca is the way it will be for me in the mighty name of Jesus. I thank you Father that my baby is a wise baby and will come to the opening of my womb at the appointed time of delivery.

Father you said by your own Word "Do I bring to the moment of birth and not give delivery? Says the Lord. Do I close up the womb when I bring to delivery? Says your God. Rejoice with my daughter and be glad for her, all you who mourn over her. For she will nurse her baby and be satisfied at her comforting breast. You will drink deeply and delight in her overflowing abundance, for this is what the Lord say's "I will extend peace to my daughter like a river and the wealth of nations like a flooding river. You will nurse and be carried on her arms and dandled on her knees" (Isaiah 66:9-11). This promise is my own Lord and I receive it from your lips, Oh loving Father. Thank you for delivering me safely and swiftly to your own glory. Wait for the Lord and He will deliver you, (Proverbs 20:22).

Chapter 10

Knowing God As Your Deliverer

In this chapter I will like to shed light on God as your deliverer, even during child delivery. I want every woman to know that even in pregnancy and childbirth; the Lord is your deliverer. I want you to know for yourself the God, who asked this question, "would I bring to the point of childbirth and not bring forth? He is the one that brings to the point of childbirth. There is no one who can deliver like God, whatever from childbirth or any life situation our God is able. Who else but the Father will give such wonderful promises as, "before she travails she gives birth" (Isaiah 65:8).

In some of these scriptures we see God's promise of deliverance

- In you our fathers put their trust; they trusted you and you delivered them, (Psalm 22:4).
- The Lord helps them and delivers them, He delivers them from the wicked and saves them, because they take refuge in him, (Psalm 37:40).
- You are my help and my deliverer; O my God, do not delay, (Psalm 40: 17).
- He shall deliver me in six troubles; yea in seven there shall no evil touch thee, (Job 5: 19).
- Call upon me in the day of trouble and I will deliver thee, and thou shall glorify me.
- Surely He shall deliver thee from the snare of the fowler, and from the noisome pestilence, (Psalm 91:3).

We can see in these bible references that each time trust is exhibited there is always a deliverance that takes place from the Lord Jesus Christ. I want you to know that this deliverance is available to you even in childbirth as you can see from the Word of God.

Proverbs 20:22 says, "Wait for the Lord and He will deliver you" I want you to know that the Lord is your deliverer and He can come into the maternity ward and aid your delivery. When the Bible talks of God as a deliverer this is what it says, "the Lord is my rock, my fortress and my deliverer, (Psalm 18:2). It also tells us the job of the ministering Angels "the angels of the Lord encamp around those that fear him and delivers them (Psalm 34:7). The angels of God can actually assist you in delivery so that you do not strike your foot against any stone.

In the bible we find many instances that our God shows up to deliver His people. In blissful pregnancy and painfree childbirth I will like you to meet God as your deliverer who can also deliver your baby for you. The dictionary says to deliver is to set free, to hand over, convey, to assist or aid in giving birth. To aid or guide, to produce the promised, desired, or expected result.

This dictionary description says a deliverer is someone who can set you free, free from what? From labour pains and difficult pregnancy. Only God is able to do that. He is also one who guides or helps to produce the promised desire or desired result. Throughout the pages of the bible we meet the Lord as our deliverer and our shield. The one who said the expectation of the righteous will never be cut short. The one who is always ready to bring us to an expected end. The only one who has the power to deliver into your arms the expected result. The one who has promised I myself the Lord I will help you. Who said if you put your trust in me you will not be put to shame. We all know the Lord is there to aid us at all times. He is there to set us free and to help us achieve our hearts desire, including giving birth without pain.

This is the example we have in the bible of God attending a delivery" And at your birth, on the day your were born your navel was not cut, nor were you washed with water to cleanse you, nor were you rubbed with salt or swaddled with bands at all. No eye pitied you to do any of these things for you; but you were cast out in the open field, for your person was abhorrent and loathsome on the day you were born. And when I passed by and I saw you rolling in your blood, I said Live! Yes, I said to you still in your natal blood, Live! I made you grow like a plant of the field. You grew and developed and became the most beautiful of jewels, *(Ezekiel 16:4-7)*.

Here we see the Lord attending a delivery and commanding a neglected child to live. We see him perform all the midwifery duties including cleaning and oiling the baby as you make this confession; Papa God will bring you to a safe and swift delivery of your baby in Jesus name.

Bible Confession

Lord I bless you and I worship you. I thank you father that this pregnancy is your workmanship. You are a faithful and mighty deliverer, the most powerful deliverer in the world. I say thank you Lord; for bowing down your ears to me and delivering me speedily of my baby; for you are my strong rock for an house of defence to save me, (Psalm 31:2). You are pleased, O Lord to come into the delivery room and deliver me of my baby on the appointed day of delivery, Oh! Lord, thank you for making haste to help me, (Psalm 40:13).

Thank you father, for delivering me out of the mire of painful labour and not allowing me to sink; in you Lord I am delivered from all forms of problems and painful childbirth, and out of the deep waters of pain in childbirth, (Psalm 69:14).

Thank you Father for pleading my cause, and delivering me, quicken me according to thy word. Thank you for sending thine hand from above. Let it nourish me, and deliver me out of great waters, from the hand of labour pains, (Psalm 144:7). For my eyes are on you O Lord. And your Word will not fail me.

The Lord is my deliverer and my strength, He has turned and delivered my baby for me, because of His unfailing love, (Psalm 6:4). The Lord himself rescues me from every attack of the enemy and brings me safely to delivery in the name of Jesus", (2nd Timothy). God has said in His Word "shall I bring to the moment of birth and not cause to bring forth? Says the Lord. Shall I who causes to bring forth shut the womb? Says your God," (Isaiah 66: 9). God has promised that He will not bring me to the moment of delivery and not bring forth a live and perfect baby for me.

My Father, my Lord and my king" thank you for keeping me Lord, and delivering my baby for me speedily; let me not be ashamed or disappointed, for my trust and my refuge are in you, (Psalm 25:20). God will never deliver me over unto the will of mine enemy labour pain, but He who bore my pain on the cross will bring me safely to a pain free delivery on my appointed delivery date in the name of Jesus, (Psalm 25:20).

"Blessed be the Lord my strength and my shield and my deliverer. My heart trusts in him, and I am helped. My heart leaps for joy and I will give thanks to him in songs. The Lord is the strength of His people, a fortress of salvation for His anointed one," (Psalm 26:6-8). Father, I thank you for delivering me from every evil work that the enemy plans during pregnancy and childbirth, and preserving me unto your heavenly kingdom; to you be glory forever and ever -amen, (2nd Timothy 4:18).

Finally the bible says "thy God whom thou servest continually, He will deliver thee," (Daniel 6:16). Thank you Father in Jesus name. Amen.

Chapter 11

Problem pregnancies uncommon in the Bible

If you read through the pages of the Bible you will discover that problem pregnancy was not a common occurrence, it was a strange thing for a Jewish woman to have problems during pregnancy. Problem in pregnancy was uncommon. Lets' take an example from the bible "Rebekah became pregnant, the babies jostled each other within her, and she said, "why is this happening to me?" so she went to enquire of the Lord," (Genesis 25: 22-23).

Rebekah had grown up to see how easy it was for her mother, aunts and female relatives to have babies that when her own pregnancy was different she went to enquire from God. In her years of marriage a lot of children had been born yet she had never seen a problem pregnancy before. This made her go to the Lord in prayer and the Lord said to her "two nations are in your womb, and two people from within you will be separated; one will be stronger than the other and the older will serve the younger," (Genesis 25: 23). The Lord made it clear to her that she was expecting twins who were already fighting even before birth in the womb, apart from that; there was nothing wrong with her pregnancy.

What of the remarkable story of Jabez? The bible tells us in 1st Chronicles 4:9, that "Jabez was more honourable than his brothers. His mother had named him Jabez, saying, "I gave birth to him in pain." From this scripture you can see that painful childbirth was not common in bible days. This mother had, had so many children blissfully. In all her relatives, friends and neighbours painful childbirth was unheard of; the pain she experienced when she gave birth to Jabez made her to name him "son of pain".

A good example of a woman who died in childbirth is Rachel and this was as a result of a curse. We shall look at her story later. So I want to encourage you to take a strong stand against problem pregnancy, for this is not part of the blessing of the covenant that we have with our Lord Jesus Christ.

Chapter 12

Problem in pregnancy

"When Laban had gone to shear his sheep, Rachel stole her father's household gods" Jacob deceived Laban - by not telling him he was running away. So he fled with all he had, "(Genesis 31:19-21). Jacob took his whole family and fled from Rachel's father.

Before they left Rachel stole her father's household gods. These gods she stole were a form of charms or idol, which were supposed to protect families and bring good fortune. These gods are the kind of things God has forbidden to be in the midst of His people. Laban (Rachel's father) pursued Jacob and finally caught up with him. "Laban said to Jacob, "What have you done? You deceived me, and carried off my daughters like captives in a war. Why did you steal my gods? Jacob answered Laban, I was afraid "But if you find anyone who has your gods**, he shall not live**. Now Jacob did not know that Rachel had stolen the gods so Laban searched all the tents and when he went into Rachel's tent "Rachel had taken the household gods and put them inside her camels saddle and was sitting on them. Laban searched throughout the tent but found nothing, Rachel said to her father, "Don't' be angry, my Lord, that I cannot stand up in your presence; I am having my period," So he searched but could not find the household gods, (Genesis 31: 26.30-35).

Here we see Rachel stealing her father's gods and opening a door for a curse to come upon her. Her husband had pronounced a curse of death upon the person who stole these gods and she did not confess or repent of stealing it. Later on she died in childbirth because of the curse that the husband pronounced on the person that stole the gods of her father. The Bible says "Rachel began to give birth and had great difficulty in childbirth the midwife said to her, "Don't be afraid, for you have another son. And she breathed her last - for she was dying— so Rachel died and was buried, (Genesis 35: 16-19). This was the end for Rachel; the curse had taken her life.

Thousands of women die every year due to problems in childbirth. Many reasons are shown and sometimes no reason is found as to the causes of these deaths. Could it be that some how, some where a curse has alighted upon their lives? These questions can only be answered individually as everyone examines himself or herself. Could a curse have alighted somewhere from disobedience to parents or spouses or someone who has authority over their life? In human social relationships, the Bible gives authority to the husband and father as the primary example of a person appointed to exercise authority. Even though there are other commonly recognised authority we will stick with this two. That of the father and the husband. God alone has absolute authority. All other forms of authority are subject to limitations of various kinds. "The head of every man is Christ, and the head of the woman is man and the head of Christ is God, *(1st Corinthians 11:3)*. And what they say into our lives matter a great deal.

Today we can shut all the doors that may have been opened by asking God to forgive us of any hidden sin and washing us clean with the blood of Jesus. Sisters get your husband to make this confession over you. I love you both.

Husband pray for your wife
I have not left out husbands completely in this book - now husbands make this confession over your wife.

Father I come to you as a husband in the name of Jesus and I bless my wife. I love her because she is your gift and blessing to me. She is the other half of me and I love her so much. I repent of any word I may have spoken into her life that could have brought a curse into her life. If there is any curse in her life I replace it with your blessings. I thank you for giving her a blissful pregnancy and safe delivery in Jesus name. Amen.

Chapter 13

Blissful pregnancy in the bible

Sarah had a blissful pregnancy and pain free childbirth at the age of 90 – 91. The Bible says "the Lord was gracious to Sarah as He had said, and the Lord did for Sarah what He had promised. Sarah became pregnant and bore a son to Abraham in his old age at the very time God had promised him," (Genesis 21:1-2).

Two women in the bible that we are told the Lord was gracious to in their pregnancies are Sarah and Hannah. Now lets look at what the bible says-

1. "And the Lord was gracious to Sarah, as He had said, and the Lord did for Sarah what He had promised," (Genesis 21:1).

2. "The Lord was gracious to Hannah, she conceived and gave birth to three sons and two daughters", (1ˢᵗ Samuel 2:21).

In these two bible verses we see two women of God that faced great challenges in their lives. To each of them the bible tells us that God was gracious to them and they conceived and gave birth to children.

If you read carefully the description of the meaning of the word **gracious** you will find that every ingredient needed for a blissful pregnancy is included in this word. The word gracious is a word that is rich with God's goodness, I will like to break this word down for you to show you that Sarah at over 90 years old and Hannah after waiting for many years had a blissful pregnancy and pain free childbirth.

In the word "**gracious**" is every ingredient needed for a blissful pregnancy. One of the ingredients of the word gracious is the word, "Kindness" which means to be disposed to be helpful and benevolent, forbearing, considerate, or compassionate, showing sympathy, cordial, friendly, not harmful, mild, gentle.

God was kind to Sarah and Hannah. He was benevolent to them. The Lord helped Hannah and Sarah. Throughout their pregnancies He was good and considerate to them. He showed them His compassion. He came into their life and alleviated all their suffering and pain. He showed them that He cared for their well being. He was cordial to these two women. His warmth and gentleness flowed out to them.

In this special time in their lives the Lord became a friend to them. He showed His goodwill and interest in their well being. He comforted and favoured them. He protected them from harm and made sure they and their babies did not suffer any physical or mental injury. He allowed no mischief to come near their tent. The Lord was at their side throughout their pregnancies and on the day of delivery He was there to make sure everything was mild and gentle for them. There were no labour pains. Every thing went peaceful and naturally for them. For Sarah and Hannah God was gracious to them and He has done the same for you. All you have to do is reach forth in thanksgiving and begin to thank him for it.

Another ingredient of the word gracious is courtesy. The Lord showed courtesy to Sarah and Hannah. And He has done the same for you. What is courtesy? It is a courteous behavior, a courteous act or expression. By courtesy of, through the kindness, generosity, or permission granted by (a person or organization). Almighty God is the person who gave these two women the best of everything throughout their pregnancies.

The third ingredient of a blissful pregnancy, still coming out of the definition of the word gracious is: Tact which means a keen sense of how to handle people or affairs so as to avoid friction or give offence. Sensitivity, perception, discernment, judgment, thoughtfulness, consideration, finesses. The Lord was sensitive to their needs, He was finely aware of the attitude and feelings of these women and would not allow them to be provoked or hurt emotionally. God was in full control of every second of their pregnancy and childbirth. He had perception of their progress and their desires. He discerned their every move and was there to hold their hand. His faithful judgement was with Sarah and Hannah during their pregnancies and child delivery. Only He could decide the outcome of their pregnancies and He decided to make it gracious for them. He was very thoughtful of their situation, having carefully considered it, he still chose to be gracious. The Lord has done the same for you.

The fourth ingredient of a blissful pregnancy still coming out of the definition of the word gracious is delicacy- in the life of these two women God did something rare or luxurious. God made sure nothing offensive or distressing came near them during their pregnancy. Delicacy is the beautiful part of the word gracious. It is the quality or state of being dainty. Frailty. Precise and refined. Avoidance of anything offensive or disturbing. Remember Sarah was 91 years at the time the Lords Word was fulfilled in her life, the Word became rare and or luxurious for her in her situation.

Another ingredient of a blissful pregnancy coming from the word gracious is Finesse- refinement, or delicacy of workmanship. Skillful, handling of a situation. The withholding of one's highest card in the hope that a lower card will take the trick, because the only opposing higher card is in the hand of an opponent who has already played. After the enemy had played his card in the life of Sarah and Hannah, God now showed the finesses of His workmanship and the grace of His power that never fails. And perfected their lives by giving them the best of everything. By skillfully handling their pregnancies and deliveries there was no emergency in both their situations. Sarah was 91 years and Hannah was carrying five babies in her womb at the same time. Both situation needed special care and the Lord was in full control. The bible says faithful is He who has promised and will do what He has promised.

Another ingredient of the word gracious is the word Elegance. God made sure these women looked elegant throughout their pregnancies. Not only did they look elegant they looked, exquisite which means to be marked by flawlessness, beauty, and delicate craftsmanship. Extremely beautiful, delightful. The Lord made sure Sarah and Hannah were looking extremely delightful and beautiful throughout their pregnancies they were on top and not beneath. Remember He was gracious to them. You are also blessed because He has already done more than this for you.

Another ingredient of the word gracious is the word Lightness. During their pregnancy He made it light for them, so that the weight of the growing babies was not so heavy on them, especially in the case of Hannah who was carrying multiple pregnancy. As you will read in a later chapter of this book. He made their pregnancies and delivery to exert minimum pressure and everything went soft and gentle for these two women. Their delivery was made easy with them putting in very little effort because the Lord was gracious to them and took away all their cares and worries.

Another ingredient of a blissful pregnancy still coming out of the definition of the word gracious is Freedom from hard work, which means the absence of necessity or constraint in choice or action. Liberation from slavery or restraint. Solid, difficult, complicated, stormy, cruel, and severe, hard labour or unremitting work, unyielding, tough, strong, dense stiff, rigid, strenuous, laborious, tiring, exhausting, back breaking, complex, complicated, baffling. The Lord freed these two women from hard work by eliminating all sickness and disease that afflict women during pregnancy. All the complications of pregnancy and the strains of labour were removed form them. He freed them from hard work.

He was gracious to them and He made sure their pregnancies and child delivery were not difficult, complicated, stormy, cruel, severe, hard or unremitting work. Do you know there are women that have gone through pregnancy and delivery and lost the child? That is what you call unremitting work. But because the Lord is gracious to you, He has freed you from every work of darkness and blessed you with a blissful pregnancy and painfree childbirth.

The Lord did it for Sarah. When God first told her she will conceive she and her husband were almost 100 years old. Abraham and Sarah laughed at God. They thought God was joking by telling geriatrics like them they would be parents, but as we see in Genesis 21, God's Word came to pass and that child was born. Hannah prayed so much that God answered her and blessed her with Samuel. But in her second pregnancy where she was carrying multiple pregnancy, God became gracious to her also and freed her from all hard work. He did it for them He has also done it for you.

Now sister make your confession that will help you change the negative image you might have formed about childbirth - to a positive one in Jesus name.

Confession

In the name of Jesus, I choose to be strong in this pregnancy and to wax strong in the Lord and in His mighty power. I am a blessed woman like Sarah and Hannah the Lord is gracious to me. My pregnancy and child delivery is free from hard work. The Lord has taken away every disease of pregnancy and childbirth from me. The power of the Holy Spirit quickens my mortal body. I am free from all kinds of sickness and disease. What the Lord has done for me is rare and luxurious. I am a woman of leisure in His presence. I have His grace and goodness in abundance throughout my pregnancy for the Lord is gracious to me. Thank you Lord. Amen.

Chapter 14

Special care pregnancies

There are certain pregnancies that doctor's regard as special care pregnancies. In special care pregnancies they will keep a close eye on you throughout your pregnancy. While the doctors are doing their part we will also use the Word of God to do our own spiritual part. As the bible says, everything works together for good for those who love the Lord. Remember that the Lord is gracious to you. The master specialist is in full control of your pregnancy and will handle it with skill.

Anaemia- there are women that are slightly anaemic before pregnancy this is usually due to iron deficiency. It is important to correct this so that you can enjoy your pregnancy and any bleeding during labour. Your doctor will prescribe iron tablets and good eating habits to build up iron in your body. You can also use the Word of God to accelerate what the food and tablet is doing in your body.

Sister you need to speak the unfailing Word of God over your body now and decree the power of God against anaemia. However you need to correct your diet and make sure you are eating the right kind of food.

Prayer

Father I bless you and I thank you. I worship you for your unchanging word. I declare my victory over anaemia and I say by your Word anaemia is far from me. I thank you O Lord that as I eat properly and take my iron tablets my iron level is normal. I will not suffer anaemia in this pregnancy or in my life in Jesus name. Amen.

Small for date babies- A baby who doesn't grow properly in the womb and is small at birth is called "a small for date" baby. The reason for this could be the diet of the mother; smoking or where the placenta doesn't work properly due to medical problem like diabetes.

Bible confession to overcome having a small for date baby

My baby will grow well in my womb. The bible says, "Jesus grew" my baby will keep growing like a tree planted by rivers of water. The quickening power of the Holy Spirit accelerates the growth of the baby in my womb. Thank you Lord. Amen.

Worrying about the birth.
One worry that a lot of women have in pregnancy is whether labour and birth will be painful and how they will cope. It is difficult to imagine what a contraction might be like and no one can tell you though many will try.

Prayer
Father I thank you that the Spirit of the Lord who planted this baby in my womb and who knows the day of my delivery, will stimulate my labour and then increase the speed of my contractions and dilation and bring me to a quick and swift delivery at the divinely appointed date in Jesus name.

Diabetes
A disorder caused by insufficient or absent production of the hormone insulin by the pancreas. Insulin is an important hormone responsible for the absorption of glucose into cells for their energy needs and into the liver and fat cells for storage. When the body is deficient of insulin

the body's glucose level becomes abnormally high causing what is called (polyuria) (the passing of large quantities of urine) and polydisia (excessive thirst). The inability of the body to store or use glucose causes weight loss, hunger and fatigue.

There two principle types of diabetes
Mellitus insulin.

- Insulin dependent (Type 1) diabetes
- Insulin dependent (type 11) diabetes

Diabetic pregnancy.

Special precautions are necessary for pregnant women who had diabetes mellitus before their pregnancy and also for those women who develop diabetes during pregnancy (this condition is known as gestation diabetes.) This is a mild form of diabetes that appears at the later part of pregnancy and disappears after the birth of the baby. The most important thing is that your blood sugar level remains stable. There are various treatments available at your clinic. Your obstetrician and antenatal clinics will be able to give you the best advice.

What we are going to do is to combine the advice of our doctors with the living Word of God, which has the power to change every situation for our good.

Bible:

A woman with diabetes can use the following confessions daily

This is the prayer I used to get rid of diabetes in my body, including total and radical change of my eating habit. Exercise became part of my daily routine and loads of vegetables. Cucumber and leeks are so helpful. In a few days my sugar level was back to normal and my weight really came down. Now use the Word of God and watch your diet carefully.

Prayer

In the mighty name of Jesus Christ I command my pancreas to secrete insulin. I command my body's glucose level to become normal in obedience to the name of Jesus Christ. I command in Jesus name that my blood sugar level become normal. The Lord is gracious to you, through His finesse, refinement, and delicacy of workmanship, His skilful handling of every situation handed to him, He has eliminated diabetics from your body in the name of Jesus. My body stores the normal amount of glucose and uses the normal amounts also. My blood is the same as the blood of Jesus Christ my Lord and Saviour. Jesus has no diabetes in His body and because He does not, I refused to allow diabetes to stay in my body. I declare that Christ bore all my pain and sickness on the cross and by His stripes I was healed. I am free from any form of diabetes. Thank you Father in Jesus name amen.

Chapter 15

Placental problems

This is the organ that nourishes the baby. As the placenta becomes fully-grown, it will attach itself to the wall of the womb and act as a filter between you and the baby. It will provide food through the blood supply and also get rid of any waste products. The umbilical cord, which attaches the fetus to the placenta has three parts: one to carry blood and nutrients to your baby; and the other two to take away waste products and blood which has had its oxygen used up. The placenta can some times cause a number of problems, which are as follows:

Abruptio placenta: this occurs when the placenta starts to shear away from the wall of the womb. It's not really known why it happens; though it tends to be more common in women who have had two or more children. The main symptom is bleeding and pain, though in mild cases there may be no more than a trickle of blood.

Placenta praevia: this happens when the placenta is embedded so low in the uterus that it partially or completely blocks the cervix, preventing the baby from being born. As the womb grows in later pregnancy, the placenta may shear away, causing bleeding and threatening the baby's oxygen supply.

Placental insufficiency: if the placenta is not working properly, the baby may be deprived of food and oxygen and may be born early and small. This may happen because the placenta has developed abnormally or failed to embed properly, or because there are blood flow problems within the placenta. The placenta may start to fail as pregnancy continues after term.

Vaginal bleeding – if you notice bleeding from your vagina at any time in pregnancy, call your doctor without delay and lie down in bed.

Bleeding in pregnancy before the 28th weeks of pregnancy could mean an impending miscarriage. After this time, it may mean that the placenta is bleeding, or the placenta has started to separate from the wall of the womb or it could be too low down in the womb, and covers, or partially covers the cervix (placenta praevia).

Pre – eclampsia: Pre eclampsia - this is one of the problems that occur in late pregnancy. About 75% of mothers to be develop pre-eclampsia, the high blood pressure disease of pregnancy. It's not really known why it happens, but it's thought that it may be due to the body rejecting the placenta as a foreign body. The first warning sign is usually a raised blood pressure above 140/190. Swollen ankles, feet, or hands or excessive weight gain and traces of protein in the urine. Now my sisters say your prayers and stand against placental problems in the name of Jesus.

Prayer

Father I bless you and I worship you, I give you glory because you love and care for me so much. Thank you O God. My God keeps my lamp burning; my God turns my darkness into light. With His help I can advance against a troop, with my God I can scale a wall. Placenta previa or pre- eclampsia there is no room for you in my pregnancy, (*Psalm 18:28-29*).

Abruptio placenta is not my portion; my placenta will not shear away from the wall of my womb. I am a blessed woman. Placenta praevia, I bind you in the name of Jesus. I am a woman of covenant; I reject any signs of you coming near my pregnancy. Placental insufficiency is far from me. The quickening power of the Holy Spirit is upon me. My placenta is working properly; my baby will not be deprived of food or oxygen or be born early and small in the name of Jesus. My placenta has developed normally and has embedded properly. The blood flow within my placenta is normal. My placenta will not fail in Jesus name. Amen.

The Lord has given plenty of room for my pregnancy to prosper and my steps under me are firm, **Vaginal bleeding** will not come near me, my baby will not slip," (*Psalm 18: 36*). The blood of Jesus speaks mercy, better and noble things than the diagnoses of the doctors. My placenta is normal, every part of my placenta functions in the way that Christ created it to function. I reject every attempt of any *placental* malfunction to come near me during my pregnancy in the mighty name of Jesus," (*Hebrews 12: 24*). Amen.

Chapter 16

Multiple birth in the bible Hannah and Rebecca

Hannah (I Samuel 1)

Many of us know the story of Hannah a great lady who loved God. She had prayed for years to have a baby. Finally, she got desperate for:

> In bitterness of soul Hannah wept much and prayed to the Lord. And she made a vow, saying "O Lord Almighty, if you will only look upon your servant's misery and remember me, and not forget your servant but give her a son, then I will give him to the Lord for all the days of his life, (I Samuel 1: 10-11).

Here we read of a desperate woman, who wanted a child. She had prayed for years without result. Finally, she decided to give back to God that which she desired most.

The Bible says that in the course of time, God remembered her. "She conceived and gave birth to a son. She named him Samuel, saying, 'Because I asked the Lord for him,'" (I Samuel 1: 20).

But remember before she got pregnant she had given that child to the service of the Lord. Now when the time came for her to fulfil her promise she was true to her word. For the bible says " when the boy was weaned, "she took the boy with her, young as he was, along with a three year old bull, an ephah of flour and a skin of wine, and brought him to the house of the Lord at Shiloh." When they slaughtered the bull, they brought the boy to Eli and she said to him:

> "As surely as you live, my lord, I am the woman who stood here beside you praying to the Lord. I prayed for this child and the Lord has granted me what I asked of him. So now I give him to the Lord. For his whole life he shall be given over to the Lord." And she worshipped the Lord", (I Samuel 1: 24-28).

This is the story of a faithful woman. God knew He could trust her. She proved herself to be faithful to Him. Even giving her son was not enough. When she went to give that son, she brought more offerings to give in the house of God. Nobody could stop her giving. She gave her best to the One who gave her what nobody could give her.

As I told you earlier, nobody can out-give God. Let us see some of the rewards of this faithful act of this faithful woman.

> Then the Lord was gracious to Hannah; she conceived and gave birth to three sons and two daughters, (I Samuel 2: 21).

We see God's faithfulness demonstrated. He blessed her with two daughters and three more sons, in one conception. This is multiple birth. Note the word here that gives us the clue "she conceived that is mentioned once, she "gave birth" that is mentioned once. Then it tells us "three sons and two daughters. Hannah gave birth to five children in one conception because God was gracious to her. What a mighty God we serve! In another chapter we will look at the word gracious and what it means when God is gracious to you.

Rebecca (Genesis 25: 24-26).

Rebecca gave birth to twins "When the time came for her to give birth, there were twins boys in her womb. The first to come out was red, and his whole body was like a hairy garment; so they named him Esau. After this, his brother came out with his hand grasping Esau's heel; so he was named Jacob," (Genesis 25: 24-26).

In both Hannah and Rebecca we see biblical examples account of multiple birth. We see clearly that these women delivered their babies without encountering any problem. This is the way God ordained it to be. Now speak the Word of God over your life sister if you are expecting twins or more. The same Lord who gave Rebecca and Hannah a blessed pregnancy has also blessed you with a blissful pregnancy and perfect delivery in Jesus name.

Prayer

God has blessed me mightily, because He loves me and I am precious to him. He has taken away my reproach and my fears and filled me with His love. I am strong in him. The Holy Spirit of God who lives in me refreshes me throughout my pregnancy with His quickening power. I am full of strength and vigour. As my babies grow, my womb will continue to grow and increase in the way ordained by God. The same Lord who kept five babies in Hannah's womb and she did not need any medical intervention has done the same for me. Multiple birth is a blessing to me and I have all of my help coming from the Lord of all the earth. There will be no complication in my pregnancy in Jesus name. Thank you Lord. Amen.

Chapter 17

Some General questions on pregnancy answered from the bible

Question 1. Veronica is there any particular place mentioned in the Bible where I can have my baby?

Where your baby is born is very important and it is a decision you must make early in your pregnancy. Most babies are born in hospital and other women opt for home birth or the GP units and domino scheme where your midwife delivers your baby in hospital.

Whatever choice you make remember the important thing is to have a healthy mother and baby at the end of the day. The bible does not recommend any particular place of birth, but we can infer that most births took place at home with the midwives in attendance. There was also the hospital system in Egypt as mentioned in- Exodus 1:16, "then the king of Egypt said to the Hebrew midwives, …when you act as midwives to the Hebrew women and see them on the birthstool" from this we can infer that it was a hospital delivery system. Pray that the Holy Spirit will guide you and lead you in His wisdom as to the best decision to make concerning choice of a place to give birth. God bless you.

Question 2. *What are braxton hicks' contractions?*

Braxton hick contractions are false contraction that tends to happen towards the last weeks of pregnancy. These contractions tend to come and go but true labour contractions occur very regularly and grow stronger and more frequently so you should be able to tell when the real labour begins.

Prayer

Now sister, make a confession against having braxton hick's contractions during your pregnancy.

In the mighty name of Jesus I reject braxton hicks contractions. Any thing false will not come into this pregnancy. The quickening power of the Holy Spirit is upon me. As my delivery date approaches the Holy Spirit stimulates my body and my womb preparing it for delivery. I choose to walk in the light of the Word of God and the Word of God shields me from falsehood. Any thing false including false contractions will not be part of my pregnancy. I thank you Father in Jesus Name. Amen.

Question *3*. Veronica, I am a smoker and I love drinking. Now that I am pregnant I want to give it up for the safety of my baby but I can't do it on my own. What help does the Word of God offer me?

I thank God that you are bold enough to confront the issue of smoking and drinking now that you are pregnant. When you smoke carbon monoxide and nicotine passes into your lungs and blood stream. This means that:
A. Your baby gets less oxygen and cannot grow as well as it should.
B. The nicotine makes your baby's heart beat faster, if you're constantly breathing other people's smoke it may have a harmful effect.

Alcohol
Heavy or frequent drinking can seriously harm your baby's development.
To be on the safe side, stop altogether. Ask the Lord to give you the grace to give up this habit.

Bible

Lets just go into the bible and hear the mind of God on this issue. We find in Judges 13:3-4, what the Lord said to Samson's mother when she was pregnant. *"You shall conceive and bear a child. Please be careful not to drink wine or similar drink and not to eat anything unclean"*. God specifically told this mother to stay away from strong drinks and anything unclean, which I know, includes cigarettes. As you have now asked for help, God himself will help you by giving you strength to overcome those habits that are not really good for you or your unborn child.

Now let us pray:

Father I bless you. I thank you that you are my refuge and my strength and my present help in trouble. Father, I refuse to fear that I will not be able to overcome this smoking and drinking of strong drink. You said in your Word I should not be filled with wine, which leads to debauchery. Instead I should be filled with your Holy Spirit according to Ephesians 5:16. I receive strength from you and the Holy Spirit and I rise above all these habits in the name of Jesus. I choose to take your yoke which is light and I cast down the yoke of slavery and bondage to bad things in the name of Jesus. From today I say goodbye to every unclean habit and I receive the grace to excel above every vice of the evil one. Christ overcame the world and gave me victory and I receive that victory in the mighty name of Jesus. Thank you Father. Amen.

Question 4. Veronica, from beginning to the end of my pregnancy, I am always sick. What does the Lord have in His Word for me to help me overcome this situation?

The reason why the enemy attacks you during pregnancy is because he knows you are ignorant of your right in God concerning childbirth and pregnancy. The enemy will act on your ignorance and try to use it to rob you of all that God has for you. God said to you in His Word "his blessing adds no sorrow" if you have to suffer throughout your pregnancy that means God's Word is a lie, but we know that the

Word of God is truth. The Word of God tells us that Christ has paid the price for all our pain and disease. Today you must take your stand against sickness in the name of Jesus.

Prayer

Christ bore the sickness on the cross for me. I need not be sick at all not even in pregnancy. The Lord has made the boundary line of life to fall for me in pleasant places I have a godly inheritance. I am blessed in the city and blessed in the field. No more sickness. I take my stand from today and I declare no more sickness in Jesus name. Amen.

Question **5**. Help me Lord, I suffer so much backache during pregnancy, what can I do?

According to most pregnancy books, backache is a problem always associated with pregnancy. According to the Word of God, your pregnancy doesn't have to be accompanied by backache. In the mighty name of Jesus my sister you must say good bye to backache.

Now let us pray: -
Goodbye backache! Christ bore my pain, He paid the full price for all my pains, Isaiah 53:4-5- tells me that Christ has carried all my pain and nailed it to the cross. He became sick with my sickness in order that I might become healed forever. I don't have to suffer backache in my pregnancy, because Christ has paid a full price for all my aches and pains, I refuse to suffer any form of pain in my pregnancy. Mighty God I worship you. You are so good Oh God. You are my father's God and it is You who helps me. Almighty God, you have blessed me with the blessings of the heavens above; blessings of the deep that lies below, and the blessings of the breast and womb. Your blessings O God are greater than the blessings of the ancient mountains, (**Genesis 49:25-26**). Thank you Lord.

I choose to walk in peace in this pregnancy. I reject backache and I command it to leave me now and never come back for by His stripes I was healed. Amen.

Question **6.** What can I do to avoid my baby being overdue?

As your delivery date approaches, every one gets excited, but often that date passes and you are still awaiting the arrival of your baby. Each day that passes now seems like ages and you may grow tired and keep wondering when it is going to be.

To avoid delays and frustration, you can start to pray now that the Lord will be with you and give you peace of mind even before the day of delivery. The bible tells us in Ecclesiastes 3:2, that there is "a time to be born," and Acts 17:26, says, "he determined the times set for them and the exact places where they should live". God has a specific date for your child to be born and our prayer is that you will not be overdue by a single day. He said in His Word "I set the appointed time," Psalm 75:1. As you pray His Word the baby will arrive at the exact day ordained by the Lord.

Prayer

Father I bless you and I worship you. I want to thank you in the mighty name of Jesus. I ask you Oh Lord to take full control of everything relating to my pregnancy. Father you know the date of my delivery. It is you who "set the appointed time". Take control and give me peace of mind and on the date set by you bring forth my baby strong and healthy in Jesus name I pray. Amen.

Question **7.** What can I do if the doctor says I should have an abortion because the baby has a congenital disorder or is not normal?

God says, "I reverse what men say and make nonsense of their wisdom, (*Isaiah 44:25*). This is what the Bible says: "Everything that God created is good and nothing is to be thrown away or refused, if it is received with thanksgiving-for it is hallowed and consecrated by the Word of God and by prayer," (*1st Timothy 4: 4*). If you have received the baby in your womb by faith that child is perfect because God's Word says so.

The Bible says:

- Every good and perfect gift is from above, coming from the Father of the heavenly lights who does not change like shifting shadows," (*James 1:7*).

- The Lord is close to the broken-hearted and saves those who are crushed in spirit," (*Psalm 34:18*).

- Which of you, if his son asks for bread will give him a stone? Or if he asks for a fish will give him a snake? If you, then, though you are evil, know how to give good gifts to your children, how much more will your Father in heaven give good gifts to those who ask Him! (*Matthew 7:9-11*).

- A righteous man may have many troubles, but the Lord delivers him from them all. He protects all his bones. Not one of them will be broken. The Lord redeems His servants; no one will be *condemned* who take refuge in Him," (*Psalm 34:17-20,22*).

- The wicked lie in wait for the righteous, to take their very lives; but the Lord will not leave them in their power or let them be condemned when brought to trial," (*Psalm 37:33*).

God has promised you this - if you are brought to trial He will not let you be condemned. When the doctor tells you, your baby is not normal and the best thing to do would be to terminate the pregnancy, the God who said in His Word that *"you shall not kill, ("Exodus 20:13*). Has promised He will not leave you in their power.

God has promised He will not let them condemn your baby to death," He says the baby in your womb is His workmanship, to declare His glory". He promises not to let your baby die, If you will agree with Him by faith, you already have victory through His son Jesus Christ. He has said in His Word that He is your stronghold in times of trouble. He is the Lord! He is your fortification and your place of refuge. Once you run to Him, He becomes your strong tower and you are safe from harm and danger. It is the Lord, Who will help you and deliver you from the wicked because you take refuge in Him,"(*Psalm 37:39-40*). Now my sister speak the Word of God. I am standing in agreement with you for His Word is truth and cannot fail you.

Your Prayer
Father I do not know how the bones grow in the womb of her with child, Ecclesiastes 11:5, but you know O Lord; I bless you that every bone in my child is perfect. According to God's Word I guard what has been entrusted to my care. This baby is my inheritance and a trust. I guard this baby with the Word of God and the Word of life that Christ has put in my mouth, (1st Timothy 6: 20). I therefore declare what Gods Word has for me: No weapon formed against me will prevail, and I refute every tongue that accuses me. This is my heritage as a servant of the Lord and this is my vindication from Him, (Isaiah 54:17).

How great is the goodness, which the Father has stored up for me because I fear him, which He has bestowed in the sight of men on me because I take refuge in Him, In the shelter of His presence He hides my baby from the intrigue of men; in His dwelling He keeps me safe from accusing tongues," (*Psalm 31: 19-20*). I do not cast away my confidence in Gods Word, because I know it will richly be rewarded. I will persevere so that when I have done the will of God, I will receive what has been promised a perfect and healthy live baby," (*Hebrews 10: 35*).

The Lord has saved my baby in accordance with His love. All men will know that it is your hand, that You, O Lord, have done it. When they attack they will be put to shame for you stand at my right hand to help me and save my baby's life from those who condemn he/her,"(Psalm *109:26-27,31*). I bless you oh Lord and I give you all the glory in Jesus name. Amen.

Question **8.** What can I do veronica? The doctor says one of my twins is not growing and must be taken from my womb?

Where the doctor says one of your twins is not growing perfectly in the womb or that your baby is not growing. At this stage it all depends on your faith. But remember the Word of God cannot fail you. Now my sister use scriptures to command the bones in your baby's body to grow. I am in agreement with you that the blessing of the Lord, which adds no sorrow, will become flesh in your life. If you need to call me, do that I am here for you. My phone number is at the back of this book.

Prayer
Father I bless you. According to Ecclesiastes 11:5, It is you who make bones to grow in the womb of a pregnant woman; I commit my pregnancy to you. The bible says in Romans 8:11, that the Holy Spirit quickens. Holy Spirit quicken the development and growth of the baby in my womb by your quickening power. Move fast O Lord and increase the rate of growth of the child in my womb. Father I ask you in the name of Jesus to protect my baby. Where there is any problem that is making it not to grow, I command growth now in the name of Jesus. Luke 1: 80 "tells me that the child grew". Father like Jesus I command that my baby's bones grow and continue to grow in the name of Jesus. By the power in the blood of Jesus Christ, I confess that my pregnancy is perfect in the name of Jesus. Every part of my body will function perfectly for the formation of the baby in Jesus name. My blood shall circulate effectively. Everything that passes from me to the baby shall be perfect for the development of the baby.

I command in the name of Jesus that every muscle, blood vessel, placenta, umbilical cord function in accordance with, (Ephesians 4:15-16). Which tells me that "Christ" is the head. From him the whole body, joined and held together by every supporting ligament, grows and builds itself up in love, as each part does its work". My baby's body is growing perfectly. The placenta is healthy and well nourished. The blood supply is perfect. I confess God's Word in Exodus 23:26, that I shall not have a miscarriage or any form of abnormal bleeding or malformation of the baby in my womb in the name of Jesus. I shall be a joyous mother of my children. My womb is fruitful. I am a fruitful vine by the sides of my husband's home. My children are like olive plants round about our table. As my baby grows, every aspect of its growth, formation and development is perfect in Jesus name. I bless you father in the Name of Jesus. Amen.

The Lord is my stronghold in times of trouble, because I know His name my trust is in Him, For He has never forsaken the righteous or those who seek Him," *(Psalm 8:9-10)*. In His great mercy He has given my baby new life, into a living hope through the resurrection of Jesus Christ from the dead, into an inheritance that can never perish, spoil or fade- through faith my baby is shielded from harm and death," *(1st Peter 1: 3-5)*.

I am protected from the lash of the tongue, and I need not fear when destruction comes, because I am anointed to laugh at destruction and famine,"*(Job 5:21-22)*. Take the entire glory, Father because you are wonderful in Jesus name. Amen.

Question 9. What of the fear of my children being born with a hereditary disease?
The Word of God is powerful and is able to override every situation or challenge we encounter in our lives.

I want to share with those women who are afraid of having a child that might be deformed or have a handicap a testimony from the prayer I have written at the end of this chapter. This is to help you, to encourage and let you know that God's Word is true.

In 1995, the Lord was teaching me on the subject of fear of having handicapped children and I was writing everything He taught me. Just as I dropped my pen, my phone rang. It was my friend Ivell down the line, telling me that her friend who was pregnant had been told that the child in her womb would be born severely handicapped as revealed by the tests at the hospital. The friend was confused as to what to do. I said to her, "I am just finishing a study on this issue. If I give you the prayer will your friend stand true to it. She said that yes, she would. So over the phone I dictated the whole prayer to her and she wrote it down for her friend.

Early in 1996 I received a phone call that the baby has been born normal, without any spot or blemish - a perfect baby boy to the glory of God.

What I want you to know is that the Word of God can and will always override every negative event that might happen in our life. The Word of God cannot only heal, it can create whatever part of the body you need or your baby needs to make it whole.

The Bible says, "the Word of God came to me saying, 'Before I formed you in the womb I knew you, (*Jeremiah 1:5*). The Bible says, *"your hand made me and formed me," Psalms 119:73*. Whose hands? God's hands. It is God who formed the child in your womb.

What does the word "form" mean? It means to give form, shape or existence to - to fashion, to give a particular shape to, or mould into a certain state or after a particular model, to bring into existence. It is God who forms us, including the child you may desire to have and you are afraid of having. The Bible says that God has arranged the parts in the body, every one of them, just as He wanted them to be, (*1st Corinthians 12:18*). What I am trying to bring across to you is this: if your trust is in the Lord and you personally ask Him for a child, then you can also trust that He knows where to put each part to bring forth a perfect child. The Word of God says that we are fearfully and wonderfully made,"(*Psalms 139:14*). The Bible says, *"every good and perfect gift comes from God," (James 1:17)*. The Bible says you will not ask for bread and God gives you a stone.

God is faithful. For those women, who may be pregnant and are told, "sorry your baby is deformed," or this or that is wrong, please, I encourage you to trust and believe God. My friend's friend did and ended up with a beautiful child. Even for those women who are afraid of having handicapped children, I encourage you to take the prayer written down and apply it in your situation and God will help you in Jesus' name to stand and be victorious.

Prayers for those women already pregnant

Father, in Jesus' name I worship you. I bless you and give you praise. Father, I come to you in Jesus' name and through the blood of Jesus Christ to ask you to protect and guide the baby in my womb. Thank you Father, that every good and perfect gift comes from you. You yourself said all that you create or created is good, *Genesis 1: 25.* I thank you, Father, that this baby already formed is your workmanship according to *Ephesians 2:10.* Father, all your works are beautiful and magnificent to behold. They are wonderfully finished. All your works are perfect, for every good and perfect gift comes from you, *(James 1: 17).*

I thank you for a perfect baby in Jesus' name. I condemn every tongue that has risen against my baby, and me in accordance with, (Isaiah *54:7).* I cover the baby in my womb in the precious blood of Jesus. Father I thank you for your blessing, I thank you Father, because you are my helper, you bless me with the blessings of the heavens above, blessings of the deep that lies below, blessings of the breast and the womb, blessings that are greater than the age-old hills, (Genesis *49: 25 – 26).* Your Word promises me peace, it promises that I will lie down and no one will make me afraid. You look at me with favour and you make me fruitful and increase my numbers, *(Leviticus 26: 6,9).* Father, this prayer saved one baby and it will save mine in Jesus' name. Amen.

This prayer can be said as often as you can until there is full manifestation of all you want.

Question 10. What about bleeding in pregnancy and bed rest?

Medical background
Bleeding is more likely to occur in some pregnancies, even though it does not inevitably mean miscarriage. Most pregnant women who experience vaginal bleeding in pregnancy still end up delivering normal live babies. The bleeding may be slight or severe. Whether the bleeding is light or heavy and accompanied by pain or not, would obviously

determine what percentage of women who bleed carry on and have a miscarriage as against those who continue with the pregnancy. Among women who bleed and are admitted to hospital, some 50-60 percent end up with a miscarriage. This is often described, as a threatened miscarriage leading to an inevitable miscarriage, where the bleeding is very heavy it is more likely to result in a miscarriage.

For more on miscarriage order my book,*"Oh God, Why All The Miscarriages?"* By Veronica Anusionwu. Published By The Lord's Word On Healing Publications @ £5.00 include £1.75 for shipping. Send your order and cheque to the address at the back of this book.

The problem now arises where a woman experience bleeding in pregnancy and ends up not miscarrying, She may start worrying if the baby will end up having a congenital disorder like spinal bifida, or down's syndrome- or cleft feet and so on. On the whole we can conclude by saying that it is normal for some women to experience very mild bleeding in pregnancy and still go on to have a healthy baby.

What about bed rest?
The most common form of "treatment" to prevent miscarriage is bed rest. At the first sign of a miscarriage women are normally advised to take things easy and rest in bed. The theory underlying bedrest is that if a woman who is prone to miscarriage lies as still or horizontal as possible, her uterus will receive the least possible stimulation thus be persuaded to hold on to the foetus.

In Britain and other countries in the world bed rest is accepted by obstetricians as an integral part of the way of treating various group of high-risk pregnancies. Women with high blood pressure, multiple pregnancies, a history of previous miscarriage or pre-term delivery may be advised to rest at home or even admitted into hospital to encourage them to rest. A lot of women prefer to stay in bed and rest as soon as any spotting or bleeding is noticed in an attempt to prevent miscarriage. The great advantage of bed rest is that it is a treatment that is relatively harmless, even though it may interfere with other activities. Another area of concern is really how much bedrest can a woman with small children get? All this issues are things that must be addressed normally.

I personally would advice a woman who is under a threatened miscarriage situation to start to speak the Word of God to her body. While she is in bed resting she can record these scriptures on a tape and play it over and over again or just spend her time confessing the Word of God so that she does not miscarry.

Other Blood related issues

High blood pressure - This is where a person's blood pressure is abnormally high. The blood pressure is likely to go up as a normal response to stress and physical activity. In a person with hypertension they will have a high blood pressure even when at rest. *Pre - eclampsia* a complication of pregnancy is a blood pressure related issue.

Rhesus problems: (*Rhesus Incompatibility*)

This is where your blood type is rhesus negative and your baby is rhesus positive. At the clinic a woman's blood is tested to see if she is rhesus positive. About 15 percent of people are negative. If you are negative you will have problems in pregnancy if you give birth to a rhesus positive baby. This is because there will be a mismatch between the blood of the mother and that of her baby, in regards to (Rh) blood group. In some cases this mismatch can lead to haemolytic disease of the newborn.

Now make your confession

I am an overcomer and I have overcome Rh incompatibility by the blood of Jesus and the Word of my testimony," (*Revelation 12:11*). My blood and my baby's blood are reconciled together by him; having made peace through the blood of His cross. Rh incompatibility is far from me in my pregnancy," (*Colossians 1:20*).

Bleeding may confront me during my pregnancy, but the Lord is my stay and my support. He has brought me and the baby in my womb into a large place; He has delivered me from bleeding because He is pleased with me and delights in me," *(Psalm 18:18-19)*.

Let everyone who is godly pray to Him while He may be found; surely when the mighty waters rise, they will not reach me, for you are my hiding-place. You protect me from bleeding and cervical erosion and disorders of the cervix and vagina and you surround me with songs of deliverance, *(Psalm 32: 6-7)*. To make His mighty power known, He has rebuked the bleeding that confronted me and it has dried up. He has saved me from the hand of the foe; from the hand of the enemy He has redeemed me. He sent His Word and healed me; He has rescued me from bleeding," *(Psalm 107:20)*.

The Lord my God has done to this bleeding, what He did to the Red Sea when He dried it up before His people. This bleeding is dried up and my baby is safe in His care. He has done this so that all the peoples of the earth might know that the hand of the Lord is powerful," *(Joshua 4:23-24)*. The eyes of the Lord are on me because I fear him, my hope is in His unfailing love, I know that He has delivered me from bleeding during pregnancy and will keep my baby alive even in famine,"*(Psalm 33: 18-19)*.

The blood of Jesus Christ the blood of the covenant has sanctified my baby and me and we are safe in His hand," *(Hebrews 10: 27)*. I am living and walking in the light, as He Himself is in the light, I have unbroken fellowship with the Lord and the blood of Christ His son cleanses, removes all sin and guilt in all forms and manifestation from me and my baby. High blood, pressure, *Pre - eclampsia* is far from me. My blood pressure is normal because it is the blood of Jesus Christ that flows in my veins. God's divine nature is my portion," *(1st John 1: 7)*. Pre – eclampsia cannot come near me in this pregnancy because of the power of the quickening power of the Holy Spirit that is upon me. I am blessed and highly favoured.

He will not let my baby slip, He who watches over me will not slumber; indeed He who watches over me will neither slumber nor sleep. The

Lord watches over me, the Lord is my shade at my right hand; the sun will not harm me by day, nor the moon at night. The Lord protects me from all harm, cervical erosion or disorders of the cervix or vagina are far from me. My God watches over my life; He watches over my coming and going both now and forevermore," *Psalm 121: 3-8.* What a Mighty Papa you are. I reverence you and give you honour for all you have done for me. Thank you Father.

Question 11

I had a premature baby and he/she is still alive what can I do for my premature baby?

Some women having miscarriage give birth to live babies. One lady shares her story- "when the baby was born he was alive and lived for forty minutes. During that time everything they did for him was done in the labour suite, which was nice as we were kept informed. *What can a mother do in this instance to help her baby?*

If a woman has a premature baby she should start confessing the Word of God which is capable of keeping the baby alive. At a time like this I know how hard it is for a woman to spend time in prayer as her mind may be in turmoil because of her experience. This confession from the Word of God will make a difference. If you are too weak, get a friend or your husband to help you confess the Word of God even one scripture is enough to save the life of your baby.

If your baby has been born premature then by the help of God that baby will live and not die.

Testimony

A friend of mine had a baby who was born premature at 26 weeks and the baby went through so much pain. One day the doctors decided that the baby could not make it and that it was time to switch off the life support machine, but my friend said no! She quickly telephoned me and told me what the doctors wanted to do. I told her I was coming to the hospital immediately. When I arrived we went into the special care unit where the baby was and we prayed over the baby and anointed him with oil in the name of Jesus. I declared that he would not die but live. The turn over was instant by the time I got home she called me to tell me that the baby was off the danger list. Today that baby is alive and healthy and making amazing progress daily. This is what you can do for your baby. Use these confessions to pray for the baby as many times as you can each day.

Confession for a premature and still born baby

Father I know that you are a gracious and compassionate God, slow to anger and abounding in love, (Jonah 4:2), in the name of Jesus I worship you. The Bible says in your hand is the life of every creature the breath of all humankind," *Job 33.4.* I put the life of my baby in your hand and I declare that my baby shall not die but live to declare the glory of God. The Spirit of God has created my baby and the breath of Almighty God gives my baby life, (*Job 33:4*). The Living Word of God preserves my baby from harm and death, (*Job 21: 21-23*). The Lord has redeemed my baby's soul from going down to the pit and my baby shall live to enjoy the light of day, (*Job 33: 4*).

My baby is growing up in Him in all things - which are in Christ, my baby's whole body, joined and held together by every supporting ligament, grows and builds itself up in love, as each part does its work, (*Ephesians 4: 15-16*).

And God says to you baby, "Live! And at your birth, on the day your were born your navel was not cut, nor were you washed with water to cleanse you, nor were you rubbed with salt or swaddled with bands at all. No eye pitied you to do any of these things for you; but you were cast out in the open field, for your person was abhorrent and loathsome on the day you were born. And when I passed by and I saw you rolling in your blood, I said Live! Yes, I said to you still in your natal blood, Live! I made you grow like a plant of the field. You grew and developed and became the most beautiful of jewels, Ezekiel 16:4-7. Yes God has spoken from His word, baby you will live and not die. I say live! Live! Live! Baby. You will live to declare the glory of God. I speak the Word of life to you baby "awake, you who sleep, arise from the dead and Christ will give you light,

(*Ephesians 5:14*).

Bible example of premature birth- Phinehas wife. (1ˢᵗ Samuel 4:22)

The wife of Phinehas was pregnant and near the time of delivery. When she heard that the Ark of God had been captured and that her father in-law and her husband were dead, she went into labour and gave birth, but was overcome by her labour pains. As she was dying, the women attending her said, don't despair; you have given birth to a son." But she did not respond or pay any attention. She named the boy Ichabod, saying, "the glory has departed from Israel," because the ark of God had been captured by the enemy and her father in-law and her husband were dead. . This will not be your testimony in Jesus name. His glory will never depart from your life in Jesus name. Amen.

Question 12-Veronica, my first baby was born with a Caesarean section, does that mean I must have all my babies this way?

Recently there was a report about how rampant caesarean section has become in the hospitals. Most doctors see this as a way out instead of normal delivery. They think it is less time consuming for them and saves them time and money. The truth is that the pain of caesarean section is greater than any thing you can imagine. You do not have to have your babies with caesarean section just because the first one was born that way. A lady attended our faith clinic whose first baby was born with C-Section. In her second pregnancy the doctors told her she had to have another C-Section because of her history. She was so worried about this. I told her to anoint her womb everyday and declare the Word of God, and all will be well, but the doctors kept on at her and finally she agreed to have the C-section. On the day of the operation the doctors could not cut through the former operation, the Lord had totally healed and sealed the place of the pervious operation. The doctor told her "you could have had your baby normally without any problems". I just want you to know that if you take your stand on the Word of God you can have normal delivery even after a C-Section.

Chapter 18

Bonding with your new baby

The hours and days following the birth of your baby are supposed to be full of absolute joy. Perfect mothers everywhere are beaming with self-satisfaction and pride looking forward to endless days of devotion to their new-born baby. But the reality can be quite different. Along with the elation there are often feelings of bewilderment and exhaustion. "Baby blues" are not uncommon and you may often feel close to tears. Sometimes looking after a new baby can all feel like too much, so you should make sure you take every opportunity to rest and don't feel too proud to accept people's offers of help. Above all, you should not feel guilty about feeling "unmaternal" at times: it is perfectly normal. Talk to other mothers, your midwife and your health visitor about your feelings.

Some women, however, find, these feelings more difficult to overcome and may find bonding with their baby particularly difficult, especially if they are suffering from postnatal depression. You can also call our ministry help line for support - you will find that you are not alone.

These are some ways to help you with this bonding process.

- Breast feeding your baby gives the perfect opportunity for lots of cuddles.
- Your baby loves skin to skin contact: skin emits special warmth

that makes him feel more secure.
- Being rocked appeals to his sense of rhythm.

Bible

Congratulations! You have just had your baby. Well-done! God loves you and has been with you through nine months of pregnancy and now has given you safe delivery of a healthy baby, rejoice in the Lord your God my sister. Pray this prayer of thanksgiving and honour to the Lord that He will help you to bond well with the new gift of life He has brought into you home.

Prayer

The Holy Sprit of God lives in me and in him is the quickening power of God, which cheers up. I call upon that power now in the name of Jesus. Holy sprit you are my cheerleader, I bless you for bringing joy into my life with the birth of the new baby. Through the power of the blood of Jesus I bond perfectly with my baby in the name of Jesus. Thank you for kindling the fire of love between me and my baby, the kind of love that comes from you Lord. Thank you for animating our relationship and making it lively and interesting. I bond with my baby perfectly in the name of Jesus. Amen.

Dealing with fatigue

The fatigue that could inevitably come with new motherhood has many causes. You have just been through a physically demanding pregnancy and birth; you are now on call 24 hours a day and you have to cope with the psychological adjustment to parenthood. To help yourself cope with this tiredness you should:

- Rest when you can. If you can afford it, get someone in to give your house a weekly make over.
- Eat a balance diet, especially if you are breast-feeding. Try to include at least some of the following at every meal; wholemeal bread, pasta, rice, potatoes, fresh fruit and vegetables, lean red meat, poultry, fish, nuts and diary products. Some women lack

energy because they have anaemia. To combat this, eat foods that are rich in iron, such as red lean meat, tuna, fortified bread and breakfast cereals, and dried fruit.

- Hand the baby over to your partner or family member or a good friend when possible, so you can have a break.
- Try to meet other mothers to share feelings and support each other.
- Don't forget your partner! It is common for men who now have to share attention with baby to become very jealous. If you can, get a baby sitter and go out, even if it's only for half an hour.
- Splash out on a treat for yourself- for example, have a relaxing aromatherapy massage or get a stylish new hairdo.

Prayer

I am not afraid because God is with me; I am not dismayed for He is my God. He strengthens me and upholds me with His right hand of righteousness, (Isaiah 41: 10).

My light breaks forth like the dawn, and my healing quickly appears; my righteousness goes before me and the glory of the Lord is my rare guide, (Isaiah 58: 7- 8). The Lord is my strength and my shield; my heart trust in him, and I am helped, Therefore my heart greatly rejoices and with songs will I praise Him for blessing me with a new baby, (Psalm 28: 7). The Lord is my light and salvation, whom shall I fear? The Lord is the strength of my life, of whom shall I be afraid? (Psalm 27:1). I am His daughter, splendour and majesty is before him; strength and joy is in His dwelling place and this is my portion from the Lord, (1st chronicles 16: 27).

I am a righteous woman, I hold onto my way, and everyday my strength grows stronger, (Job 17: 9). I thank you Lord in Jesus name. Amen.

Chapter 19

Physical activity and diet and cravings during pregnancy

Exercise

We all know that exercise is good for us. It keeps us fit and slim, release feel good endorphins, and makes for a healthy heart and body. And provided you follow a few sensible precautions, exercising regularly throughout your pregnancy is great for both you and your baby.

The key to exercising in pregnancy is maintaining fitness, rather than following a strict regime. Even if you have never exercised before, now is the ideal time to start. Not only will it give you a lift, but doing it regularly will also give you extra energy, relieve stress and anxiety, and give you strength and energy that go with carrying an extra person around in your belly.

With regular exercise, you should find that some of the symptoms of pregnancy are alleviated, such as cramps, backache and constipation and sleeplessness. Most women who exercise find it easier to regain their figure after the birth.

Your diet during pregnancy
It was believed many years ago that a pregnant woman eats for two

people. Therefore she eat large quantities of food, quite irrespective of whether it was meat, vegetables, bread, cheeses or anything else. The food to which she was accustomed was taken in increasing amounts. Today however a lot of things have changed. Many health books are on the market giving valuable advice on diet and exercise for the pregnant woman, on how best to nourish herself and her unborn baby. Each woman in her own naïve environment will be able to discern what is healthy and right and what she enjoys eating and eat it in moderation.

Water is very good and helps metabolism. A lot of vegetables, protein and fish are very good. Lean meat in moderation and carbohydrates are energy giving and can be found in sweets, flour, sugar and potatoes and milk. Iron is good and you can obtain this in your diet or take iron supplements as recommended by your doctor.

What about cravings in pregnancy?

If you find yourself in pregnancy serving cream on your biscuits, searching for wet kaolin to smell or munching on lime scale out of the kettle you are not alone. No one really knows what causes cravings in pregnancy, over half or all pregnant women report them, which is fine as long as they are not eating something potentially harmful- or not nutritious enough for you and your baby.

On the positive side many women crave fruit and dairy products. 'But that could be partly driven by the feeling that they should be eating more of these foods and boost their health when pregnant. What ever your cravings may be at this time make sure it is healthy and God will see you through.

Chapter 20

Get rid of depression

The term "postnatal depression" is just one of a group of illness which can afflict women after birth. They range from the temporary "fourth day blues" at one end of the spectrum to a full scale mental break down.

The symptoms are:
· Depression
· Anxiety
· Sleeplessness
· Lack of appetite
· Exhaustion.

Sufferers may also have no interest in things they usually enjoyed; they feel inadequate and guilty and fear they don't love their baby properly; they think they are incapable of being a good mother.

Antenatal depression

This is depression that has nothing to do with any physical problem at all. The sufferer feels like they are going mad. They could cry constantly for no reason. They could panic easily about having a baby and their ability to cope or even be a good mother. This kind of depression will normally lift after the birth of the baby.

Mood swings

This is where a pregnant woman's mood is constantly changing all the time. The first thing to do is make sure you are getting enough rest time to yourself and you have someone to talk to. The second thing we will do is use the Word of God to over come this mood swings.

The Bible

Think positive, the bible says "anxiety in the heart of a man causes depression, but a good word makes it glad". It's amazing what power effect the mind can have on the body and if you can change the way you think, you often can change the way you feel. The Word of God tells us that a good word makes the heart glad and deals with depression. Now let's use the Word of God to stand against depression.

Mood swings, antenatal and postnatal depression is not my portion "Comfort, yes, comfort my daughter!" speak comfort to yourself, cry out oh my daughter "my warfare is ended". God has given me victory; I am a happy mother of a live and healthy baby. I hold my baby in my arms and I celebrate the gift of life that the Lord has given me. I am blessed and highly favoured, I reject this feeling of rejection and feeling unloved. I know that God loves me, my husband and my family love and care for me. I receive that Comfort from you Lord. Thank you for renewing my strength Oh Lord and a steadfast spirit within me.

Because God has promised "he will never leave me or forsake me, I know He is with me always and cares about me. God calls me the apple of His eyes and that makes me special. God has engraved and tattooed me on the palms of His hand. I am mighty special and I refuse to be afraid of any thing that will come my way. I am blessed and highly favoured by God. My pregnancy is blessed and joyful. I reject antenatal depression and mood swings in the name of Jesus. The joy of the Lord is my strength. Thank you Lord. Amen.

Chapter 21

Looking good and feeling good

Reading through the pages of the bible, I believe that God actually designed His Word to give women all round beauty in pregnancy and childbirth. The bible says in Micah 2:7 "do not my words do good to him whose ways are upright? I know that God wants you to blossom throughout your pregnancy and go on to have a painfree delivery because you are an upright woman. He wants His Word to do you good. So allow the Word of God to soothe away signs of tiredness and stress accumulated throughout the day. This is your bedtime beauty routine.

Bedtime beauty - Speak the Word of God last thing at night and let Him restore your skins natural moisture balance. As you speak the Word last thing at night your skins natural defences will hear the voice of its creator and be recharged. You will wake up with your whole body enveloped in a heavenly well being. On waking up your skin and body will feel refreshed and fully recharged. Night after night your skin becomes resilient (able to recover form and position and elastically) because of His restoring word.

Now use the Word of God to enhance your beauty during this precious time in your life in Jesus name. Remember blissful means "heavenly or complete happiness during pregnancy". Now speak His Word my beautiful sister.

Your eyes and nose - My eyes are like the pool of Heshbon by the gate of Bath Rabbim. My nose is like the tower of Lebanon, which looks towards Damascus, (Song of Songs 7:3-4).

Teeth and lips and mouth - My teeth are like a flock of Sharon ewes, which have come up from the washing, of which all are in pairs, and none is missing among them. My lips are like a thread of scarlet, and my mouth is lovely, (Song of Songs 4:2,3).

Cheeks and neck - My cheeks are like halves of a pomegranate behind my veil. My neck is like the tower of David, built for an arsenal, where on hang a thousand bucklers, all of them shields of warriors, (Song of Songs 4:4).

Breast - My two breasts are like two fawns, like twins of a gazelle that feed among the lilies, my husband is satisfied by them, (Song of Songs 4:5).

Your hair and Skin - How fair I am, how beautiful are my skin and hair and my strength in this pregnancy. My eyes are like those of a dove; my hair is like a flock of goats descending from mount Gilead, (Song of Songs 1:15, 4:1). The Bible complements the skin and beauty of Absalom and I declare in the name of Jesus that from the top of my head to the sole of my feet there is no blemish. The hair of my head is like Absalom's which weighed in two hundred shekels by the royal standard, (2nd Samuel 14:25-26). I have long beautiful and healthy hair throughout my life.

My flesh is renewed like a child's it is restored as in the days of my youth, (Job 33:25). I am full of youthful vigour and it fills my bones, (Job 20:11). The splendour, which the father has given me, makes my beauty perfect, (Ezekiel 16:14). I am resplendent with light, more majestic than mountains rich with game. I am a blessed woman. I love you Lord and I worship you for your Word because it has done me good in the name of Jesus.

Chapter 22

Love making during pregnancy

God is the greatest lover you can ever find. I had difficulty understanding the book of songs of songs in the bible. One afternoon as I took a short break from my work, the Holy Spirit told me to read Song of Songs. As I read I discovered powerful scriptures to help us revive and renew our love life. In less than two hours I had written a book. I have just taken some of what the Holy Spirit taught me that day and included it in this chapter to enable you to read and apply his Word and enjoy love making during your blissful pregnancy. Remember we are doing it the heavenly way this time. Love making during pregnancy is quite normal. And there is nothing to worry about. The baby is cushioned and protected by the bag of fluid surrounding him, so there is no way lovemaking can cause any harm.

I believe there is something special and beautiful about pregnancy. During pregnancy your breast starts to grow as they gear up for breast feeding, your nipples will grow darker in colour, this acts as a sexual signal making them more attractive to your husband. You find that as you grow bigger, your hair will shine, your skin will be glowing and you will have a general feeling of bliss and contentment.

God wants you at this time to look gorgeous and delicious for your husband. Touching, kissing and cuddling is just wonderful and I believe the following scriptures from the word of God will help to revive and inspire your marriage during this wonderful time in your life.

Confession Prayer for her

The Holy Spirit of God that lives in me has quickening power and I begin to use my lips to call upon His quickening power during this time in my life. Holy Spirit kindle a fire of romance between my husband and me during this time in our life.
Stimulate our intimacy to a blissful level throughout my pregnancy. I will captivate and ravish his heart. My love will be better to him than wine. The fragrance of my body will be more pleasurable to him than spice. My lips drop honey as the honeycomb, honey and milk are under my tongue, and my kiss will satisfy him always. The odour of my garment is like the odour of Lebanon, (Song of Songs 4: 9- 11).

My husband is captivated by my love. My stature is like those of the palm and my breast like a cluster of fruit. As we climb into our bed, and he takes me into his arms, my breast will be to him like the cluster of the vine, the fragrance of my breathe like apples, and my mouth like the best wine, (Song of Songs 7:6-9).

Because of the stimulating power of the Holy Spirit who lives in me, my fountain is springing up as a well of living water and the flowing streams of Lebanon. I pray that the north cold wind and the soft south wind will blow upon my garden, that it's spices may flow out in abundance for my husband in whom my soul delights. Let my beloved, my husband come into his garden and eat his choicest fruits, (Song of Songs 4:15-16). Father I thank you for giving me the best of all that you have and I worship you in Jesus name. Amen.

Prayer for husbands but wives can join in also for desire and beauty

The Lord my God is robed in majesty and is armed with strength, because we are His children and precious to him, He has clothed us with His majesty and armed our love life with His strength, (Psalm 93: 1). ??His splendour, beauty and strength are upon our marriage, (Psalm

96: 6). The Lord has enabled me to come to my garden, to my sister, my bride; I have gathered my myrrh and my spice. He has enabled me to eat my honeycomb and my honey; I have drunk my wine and my milk, (Song of songs 5: 1). Every night I kiss my wife with the kisses of my mouth, for my love for her is more delightful than wine. Pleasing is the fragrance of her perfume; her name is like perfume poured out, (Song of Songs of 1: 1-3).

She in her pregnancy is to me like a sachet of myrrh resting between her breast. She is like cluster of henna blossoms, (Song of Songs 1:13-14). My pregnant wife delights to sit in our shade, and my fruit is sweet to her taste. I have taken her to the banquet hall and my banner over her is love. Strengthen us with raisins; refresh us me with apples, for we are faint with love. My left hand is under her head, and my right hand embraces her. I arouse and waken my penis because I desire her, (Song of Songs 2:3-7). I say to my beautiful one, come with me, See! The winter is past, the rains are over and gone. Flowers appear again on the earth; the season of singing has come, the cooing of the doves is heard in our land. The fig tree forms its early fruits; the blossoming vines spread their fragrance. Arise; come, my darling; my beautiful one, come with me, for our bed is verdant, (Songs of songs 1:17, 2:10-13). We give you worship oh Lord in Jesus name. Amen.

Chapter 23

20 Ways to pamper yourself

1. **Freshen up your make up**-If you are feeling radiant and blissful, new colours will make you feel even more so; if you are at that early blessed stage of pregnancy or in the later stages and feeling even more blessed, changing your make up will give you a boost. Cosmetic counters in departmental stores often do free makeovers, to show you how to use new colours to their best advantage, and many will also give you free samples so you can try them at home.

2. **Watch a good film**-On a chilly afternoon, snuggle up on the sofa with a warm blanket and a cup of hot milk, and watch a nice movie on video or TV. If you are on maternity leave, take yourself to a nice movie at the local cinema. Get your popcorn and drinks and get going sister. God is not a killjoy you can watch a nice movie and relax in the name of Jesus.

3. **Go for a walk with your sweet heart or a friend** -taking a walk through the park and crunching through fallen leaves can be great fun. The fresh air will put a glow in your cheeks and you will have a laugh as you remember your childhood or precious memories of the goodness of God. I used to take a nice book to the park when I was pregnant or my Walkman and enjoy nice music in the park. The bible tells us in Genesis 2:8 "the man and his wife heard the sound of the Lord God as He was walking in the cool of the day, and they hid from the Lord God among the trees in the garden. This is a park setting in the bible. God loves it and it is a good place to go and relax at times to commune with the Lord.

4. **Massage is good for you**- a neck or leg massage is wonderfully relaxing and will make you feel great. Buy some of our anointing oil or beauty oil from the Lord's Word on healing ministries and get your partner to massage you. Your friend can also do it and where you have older children you could teach them how to massage you. There are very good massage books on the market.

5. **Take a trip to the beach**- tripe to the local beach is wounderful for you and you can walk barefooted on the beach when the weather is mild enough to let you paddle on the sea or on a springy, well cut lawn. You foot will feel good and so will you.

6. **Swimming is lovely** – swimming is fun and relaxing, and helps you to keep fit at the same time. The water will support your bump, so you won't feel the weight. Some antenatal classes offer swimming classes and they are wounderful. If your offer such courses go for it. You will meet other women and make new friends and also enjoy yourself.

7. **Have a lie in** – sometimes it is good to just chill-out and have a lie in. stay in bed and listen to nice music or read a good book or your bible. You can even listen to the bible on tape. This is nice and relaxing for you and your baby.

8. **Treat yourself to something yummy**-Out of season or exotic fruits, such as strawberries, nectarines, and mangoes are delicious. They also feel a luxurious treat and are healthier than chocolates. The bible puts it this way "strengthen me with raisins, refresh me with apples, for I am faint with love," Song of Songs2: 5. (she laughs)

9. **Enjoy breakfast in bed**- make this treat really special by using a pretty tray-cloth and putting a rose in a vase to go with your favourite breakfast. Get your sweetheart to prepare it and serve it while you relax in bed. This will make you feel spoiled and well cared for.

10. **Go shopping**- shopping with a friend or another expectant mother can be fun. Both of you can coo over the baby clothes and have fun with the Holy Spirit. You can end up having lunch at a posh café. It will not cost much more than the local sandwich shop and you can enjoy being waited on.

11. **Have a healthy cocktai**l- get your partner or friend to make

you a lovely non-alcoholic cocktail. Try a raspberry Kiss (150ml cranberry and raspberry juice, 25ml orange juice and a dash of lime juice, served with ice and soda water) or a cranberry spritzer (100ml cranberry juice and 50ml white grape juice over crushed ice, with a dash of soda water and a sprig of mint).

12. **Have a long bath**- this is the perfect place for serious pampering. Treat yourself to some posh bubble bath. Some lovely bubble bath from the body shop or any good shop will be wounderful. Natural seaweed extracts will make your skin feel soft and lovely. As you walk out of the bath, you will hear him say this " how much more pleasing is your love than wine, and the fragrance of your perfume than any spice," (Song of Songs 4:10). Give yourself a candle lit dinner. A small box of chocolate or cool non-alcoholic drink will make the treat complete.

13. **Spend it on yourself**- some many women and mothers spend on every one except on themselves. Now that you are pregnant treat yourself to something you fancy particularly something you will not normally buy. Anything from a bunch of flower, beautiful maternity underwear's or clothes or even an electric toothbrush will do, just make sure you are buying it for yourself. You are beautiful and you deserve it. The bible puts it this way "the fragrance of your garments is like that of Lebanon," (Song of Songs 4:11).

14. **Give yourself a home facial**- once you have cleansed and toned your face, make yourself a moisturising mask. Mix two tablespoons of honey with two teaspoons of milk, smooth it over your face and leave it for ten minutes before rinsing it off with warm water. This will leave your skin as soft as a queen which is what you are. Remember sister, You are a chosen lady, a royal priesthood, a holy nation, and a lady belonging to God. You are a precious vessel in the hand of a mighty God, (1st Peter 2:9).

15. **Get some one to clean the house**- you may find it difficult to reach those awkward dusty corners, especially in the late stages of pregnancy. Instead of worrying about it, call a cleaning agency. They will send some one to clean your house from top to bottom for about £20, and they are also insured against breakages.

16. **Visit an art gallery**- feed your senses for an afternoon. Wandering around looking at pictures can be very relaxing, and

there are usually chairs in every room so you can sit down and take a long look at your favourite picture or have a rest.

17. **Have a romantic weekend away**- for the ultimate pampering experience; spend a weekend away with your sweetheart. Hotels often do special deals at weekend breaks, and this will give you both some precious times together before the baby arrives. Where you have older children take them to a friend or relative while you go away for the weekend. There are some hotels that have leisure centres and health spas, and some may even throw in flowers, and chocolates for an early celebration. As you go away take this scripture for the ultimate weekend experience" awake north wind, and come south wind, blow on my garden; that its fragrance may spread abroad. Let my lover come into his garden and taste its choice fruit",(Song of Songs 4:16)

18. **Get a new hair cut or hair do**- a new hair do is so wounderful and refreshing especially toward the end of your pregnancy. This makes your hair easy to manage after the baby arrives. This also refreshes you and makes you look good. So go for it sister, the Lord says "your head crowns you like Mount Carmel. Your hair is like royal tapestry; the king is held captive by its tresses. How beautiful you are and how pleasing, O love with your delight, (Song of Songs 7:5-6). This is the Word of the Lord to you, woman of God.

19. **Get a home pedicure**- remove any nail varnish from your finger nails and toes, soak your feet in warm water for 5-10 minutes, then smooth away any rough skin with a pumice stone. Dry your feet, and cut your nails straight arose with clippers, smoothing the edges with an emery board. Massage your toes and nails with almond oil or our anointing oil, then buff your nails. This will stimulate the circulation to strengthen your nails, as well as making them shiny, finally apply a clear base coat, two coats of varnish and a clear protective topcoat. If your bump is too big to allow you to reach your feet, ask a friend or your husband to do it for you. My husband used to do it for me when I was pregnant. The Lord says it this way " I arose to open for my lover, and my hands dripped with myrrh. My fingers with flowing myrrh on the handles of the lock, (Song of Songs5: 5). Your beautiful pedicure nails

will surely make an impact on him.

20. **Attend our blissful pregnancy faith clinic**- at the Lord's Word on healing ministries blissful pregnancy faith clinic we pamper our mothers. Once every six weeks you can come in and join other mothers to learn how to enjoy your pregnancy the biblical way, love making, breast-feeding and how to prepare for your delivery without pain. You will hear from our midwife about exercise during pregnancy and diet and many other issues relating to childbirth. You can even join in some excise classes if you want. There will be music and advice and even how to enjoy your bible and prayer times during pregnancy and after delivery. I look forward to meeting you there.

Chapter 24

The flight into the bottom of the sea

Suppose one of you has a hundred sheep, and losses one of them, does he not leave the ninety-nine in the country and go to look for the one that wandered off? And if he finds it, I tell you the truth, he is happier about the one sheep than about the ninety- nine that did not wander off. In the same way your father in heaven is not willing that any of these little ones should be lost,".... (Luke 15:4-7).

In this parable our Lord Jesus talks about the love that is in the heart of the Father God for you. Just like the shepherd the Father will not give up on His search for each and every one of us that has not yet returned home to him. In this very chapter we are going to be discussing the Salvation of your soul.

The Holy Spirit has used me as a vessel to write this restoration and healing book on pregnancy and painfree childbirth. This book is written by the Holy Spirit to glorify Jesus and to bless you. Going beyond the blessing we will receive, let's talk about your soul

The Bible says, "what shall it profit a man if he should gain the whole world and lose his soul? I pray that the Spirit of God will help you to receive Jesus Christ as the Lord of your life, so that not only will you be blessed here on earth with children, but have the assurance of spending eternity with Him. Many people say Oh! I am rich and I don't think God can do anything for me. Lets look at the story of one of the-:

At the age of 38 he was one of the richest men in the world. A son of a president, young and handsome with a beautiful wife by his side. He had everything to live for. On Friday 16th July 1998, He was on his way to his cousins wedding and due to delays he missed his flight. He now made a decision to fly his own private plane. He quickly rushed through his pre-flight checks, reviving up his engines in a practice area to save time. He boarded his own private plane with his wife and her sister and they took off for the wedding not really knowing that this was the final flight of their life. In mid air the plane disappeared into the sea. After three days extensive search all three were discovered under the bottom of the sea. As the people of America mourned with this great family I was forced to write this chapter for my readers who may not know the Lord Jesus Christ.

Today if you set out on a journey in your car, plane or even in a bus are you guaranteed any safety? I have since discovered that the only security we have in the world is the only security that comes from knowing the Lord Jesus as your Lord and personal saviour. The bible says, "unless the Lord guides those that guide, guide in vain". The three young people that died had a bright future ahead of them, and yet like a thief in the night death came in and stole their very young lives away from them. Were they saved? That I cannot answer. But for you my reader you can answer for your self. Are you saved? Do you know Jesus as the Lord and saviour of your life? If the roll call came for you toady will you spend eternity with Christ? Do you have an assurance that your life is right with God? Please take a moment to reflect on what you have just read and the take time to make a personal decision to know Christ for yourself.

Someone may say, "I don't believe in God or heaven or hell" the truth is that ignorance of the law is no excuse. Whether you believe in the existence of God or not does change the truth that there is a God who loves you and yearns for you. If you ignore the traffic signs you could end up having an accident. So the best thing is always to exercise caution and use the mind that God gave you to make right decisions. If you are not sure of what you are reading why not open your mouth and ask God to reveal himself to you if he is real. To find out how you can make Jesus your Lord and personal Saviour read on for salvation. If there is any thing you want us to know or pray with you please write, to the address at the back of the book.

MAN ABUSES THE WILL TO CHOOSE

God created Adam from the dust of the ground and he became a living being. Now God planted a garden in the east, in Eden and there he put the man he had formed and the Lord God made all kinds of trees grow out of the ground - trees that were pleasing to the eye and good for food. In the middle of the garden were the tree of life and the tree of the knowledge of good and evil. *The Lord God took the man and put him in the Garden of Eden to work it and take care of it. And the Lord commanded the man, "You are free to eat from any tree in the garden, but you must not eat from the tree of the knowledge of good and evil, for when you eat of it you will surely die" (Genesis 2: 7-9, 15-17).*

God created Adam with a unique ability to choose. He gave him free will and told Adam specifically, *"You are free to eat from any tree in the garden but you must not eat from the tree of knowledge of good and evil, for the day you eat of it you will surely die" (Genesis 2: 17).*

WHAT KIND OF DEATH WAS GOD TALKING ABOUT?

This was not physical death but spiritual death. Yet Adam did not obey God, for the Bible records that Adam and his wife ate of these fruit that God had commanded them not to eat. *"When the woman saw that the fruit of the tree was good for food and pleasing to the eye and also desirable for gaining wisdom, she took some and ate of it. She also give some to her husband, who was with her and he ate of it."* (**Genesis 3:6**) That disobedience brought death to the whole of mankind - why? - Because we all were in Adam when he disobeyed God's instruction. You say: "How can that be possible?" Medically, it is a fact that a man produces ten million sperm cells a day in his testicles and each of these sperm is genetically unique. So in just six months only one man produces enough sperm to populate the whole world.

There is no doubt from the Bible account, that it is, *"from one man that God made every nation of men, that they should inhabit the whole earth and He determined the times set for them and the exact place where they should live."* (**Acts 17:26**) There are a lot of theories about the origin of man but the Bible does not speculate on this issue. It is clear and simply written down for those who desire to know the truth.

After Adam's fall, we all fell with him because we all were in him. There was no other way for mankind to be saved again because the law requires that everything be cleansed with blood because without the shedding of blood, there is no forgiveness. (**Hebrews 9: 22**) Jesus came into the world, led a sinless life in the world, and He shed His sinless blood on the Cross as an offering to redeem us from the sin committed by Adam.

The Bible says therefore, just as sin entered the world through one man, and death through sin, and in this way death came to all men, because all sinned - for before the law was given, sin was in the world. But sin is not taken into account when there is no law. Nevertheless death reigned from the time of Adam to the time of Moses, even over those who did not sin by breaking a command, as did Adam, who was a pattern of the one to come. But the gift is not like the trespass, for if many died by the trespass of the one man, how much more did God's grace and the gift that came by the one man, Jesus Christ, overflow to the many! (**Romans 5: 12-16**).

Adam brought sin into the world; Jesus brought the Grace of God into the world. Jesus came into the world, died on the Cross, shed His sinless blood on the Cross to redeem you and me from the sin committed by Adam. In His death He paid the price for the sin of all mankind; the curtain of sin that separated us from God was removed forever; Christ took our place and paid the price for you and me. God sent Jesus Christ. Mankind had fallen into sin and rebellion. Mankind had turned his back on God. *"We all like sheep, have gone astray. Each of us has turned to his own way."* (**Isaiah 53: 6**) No man sought God any more; sin had separated us from God. God had to do something to restore the fellowship between him and man. This made him send Jesus to come down to the earth and die on the Cross-to redeems us from sin and death.

You and I have been redeemed from the law of sin and death. The only problem left is the one of choice; will you say yes to Christ today? His arms are wide open and waiting for you to fall into them so that He can love you and hug you. Accept Him now.

SALVATION

To accept him as your Lord and Saviour the Bible says that the Word is near you: It is in your mouth and in your heart; that is the Word of faith we are proclaiming that if you confess with your mouth "Jesus is Lord", and believe in your heart that God raised him from the dead you will be saved. For it is with your heart that you believe and are justified, and it is with your mouth that you confess and are saved. When you confess Jesus as Lord and Saviour you can pray in your own way, any way you know how, the simpler the better; the most important thing is your heart's condition.

CONFESSION

Father, I come to you in the name of Jesus. I confess that I have sinned against you and lived in sin. Father, I repent of my sins and by your power I will no longer be a servant of sin. Father; make me your child. I believe that Jesus died on the Cross and that He shed His blood for me and that He rose from the dead on the third day. I confess and accept the Lord Jesus as my Lord and Saviour. Lord; come into my life. Give me New Hope and power to live for you. Wash me with your blood and sanctify me with your Word and fill me with your Holy Spirit, to your praise and glory. Father, I thank you for making me your child. In the name of Jesus Christ of Nazareth, Amen!

RIGHT STANDING WITH GOD

Immediately after the confession you now have a right standing with God. The Bible says once we are justified through faith, we have peace with God through our Lord Jesus Christ, through whom we have gained access by faith into this grace in which we now stand. And we rejoice in the hope of the glory of God. Accepting Jesus as Lord, the Bible says, *"as many as receive him, to them He gave the power to become the sons of God, even to them that believe in His name," **John 1: 12.*** Once you have accepted Jesus Christ you now have a right standing with God and you are now born of the Spirit. This is the new birth; it gives you right standing with God. You now need to find a good church and start growing in the grace of God.

You can write to me if you want, or come to the faith clinic if you need some one to stand with you by faith to know more about your love walk with the Lord. Look for a good church and start growing in the grace of God. Whatever you choose to do the most important thing is you growing in the grace of our Lord Jesus Christ. I love you.

Chapter 25

Prayer Points

Let's repent before God of the sin of not worshipping him enough
1. Acknowledge the ministry of the Holy Spirit in your life
2. Confess before God of any sin in your life that can hinder the blessing of God from flowing in your life today
3. Now thank God for His promises that what ever you ask the father in His name He will do it for you so that the Father may receive all the glory
4. Now hold up the blood of Jesus against
5. The spirit of waste like (miscarriage- still birth deformed child etc)
6. The spirit of death, hell, accident and infirmity
7. The spirit that wastes life in the noonday lights
8. The spirit of set back and sorrow
9. Thank God for choosing both your midwife and your obstetrician in the name of Jesus
10. Worship God because all those that will attend to your delivery will be anointed by the Lord
11. Reject all headaches and pain in the body during your pregnancy
12. Declare in the name of Jesus, that all your blood tests will return normal
13. Praise God that in the name of Jesus your cervix, womb and everything will be perfect.
14. Praise God that ectopic pregnancy will not come near you in the name of Jesus
15. Praise God that there will no pain in your lower abdomen in Jesus name
16. Worship God that anaemia, backache or constipation and cramp will not come near you in Jesus name
17. Worship God because faintness, piles, heartburn and sleeplessness will not come near you in Jesus name
18. Reject tingling in the fingers and varicose veins in Jesus name
19. Worship God that in the name of Jesus your baby's head will fit

snugly into your pelvis and pass smoothly down your birth canal

20. Praise him because you know in the name of Jesus that your placenta and cord will be in the right position and not cause any obstruction
21. Reject, heartburn and itching in the name of Jesus
22. Reject Caesarean and breech position baby in the name of Jesus
23. Praise God that, leg cramps, nosebleeds and palpitations will not come near you in the name of Jesus
24. Praise God that the tissues of your vagina will be loose and soft to deliver your baby smoothly
25. Command during your delivery for strong and rapid contractions without pain
26. Reject every form of distress or abnormalities in your baby's heart beat
27. Command that your cervix will be fully dilated during delivery by the quickening power of the Holy Spirit in the name Jesus.
28. Thank God that your pelvic floor will be relaxed in the name of Jesus
29. Praise God that you will not suffer any form of bleeding in your pregnancy in the name of Jesus.
30. Reject incompetent cervix in the name of Jesus
31. Thank God because you know you will carry your baby to full term in the name of Jesus
32. Praise him because you know you will not experience any tear during your delivery
33. Praise God that your perineal skin will be moist and stretchy to allow your baby's head to pass through your birth canal
34. Praise God that you will not experience any damage to your sexual function
35. Worship God that no incontinence will come near you
36. Praise him because you know no form of placental problems will come near your pregnancy in the name of Jesus
37. Reject Rhesus problems in the name of Jesus
38. Reject pre-eclampsia in the name of Jesus
39. Praise him because you know you will not need blood transfusion
40. Worship him because you believe that the power of the blood of Jesus has separated you from the sin of your ancestors in Jesus name
41. Praise him because you know any evil dedication placed upon your life at birth will not prosper in Jesus name

42. Praise him because you know all demons associated with evil dedication has been destroyed by God's fire in Jesus name
43. Worship him because He has corrected any disorder that may be in your reproductive organs, like your placenta or cervix or your blood in Jesus name
44. Give him worship for activating your womb by His quickening power today and preparing it for a swift delivery in Jesus name
45. Thank him because no devourer will devour the fruit of your womb in Jesus name
46. Now command every form of pain in your body to cease in Jesus name
47. Dismiss and disband from your heart every thought, image or pictures of failure on these matter in the name of Jesus
48. Thank you Lord for helping me to identify and deal with any weakness in me that can hinder the manifestation of my miracle in Jesus name
49. I receive the mandate to put to flight every enemy of my breakthrough in the name of Jesus
50. Thank you father for making me a joyous mother of children
51. I take my stand against the following:
· Blood pollution.
· Parental curses.
· Marital disgrace.
· Open curses and threats.
· Spiritual abortion.
· sexual intercourse in my dream.
· Infirmity.
· Rejection.
· Now start to bless God for His goodness to you.

Now you can renew your strength with the Word of God. The bible says "the righteous will flourish like a palm tree, they will grow like a cedar of Lebanon, planted in the house of the Lord, they will flourish in the courts of our God. They will still bear fruit in old age, they will stay fresh and green, proclaiming, "the Lord is upright, He is my Rock, and there is no wickedness in him," (Psalm 92:12-15). Can you better the Word of God? You see, His promise is clear. Women who trust in Him will flourish in their pregnancy and after their delivery. Now relax and enjoy your daily confession.

Chapter 26

General Daily Confession.

*F*ather, I kneel before you, for it is from you that all the families in heaven and on earth derive their name. I pray that out of your glorious riches, you may strengthen me with power through your Spirit in my inner being throughout my pregnancy that Christ may dwell in my heart through faith. I pray that as I am rooted and established in your love, I have power to continue to blossom throughout my pregnancy. I thank you Lord for a pain free childbirth and I believe this with all my heart, because your Word is able to do immeasurably more than I can ask or imagine, according to your power that is at work within me. To You be glory forever and ever. In this pregnancy I am filled with divine goodness to the measure of your fullness O Lord, (Ephesians 3:14-21).

I thank Christ Jesus our Lord who has given me strength, that He considered me faithful, appointing me to His service, to be a mother and a co-worker with him, 1st Timothy 1:12. God said I would be saved through childbearing, if I continue in faith, love and holiness with sobriety. I choose to continue in love and holiness in the name of the Lord Jesus, 1st Timothy 2:15. I receive peace from the God of peace now and in everything including my pregnancy and child-birth, (1st Thessalonians 2: 16).

I am a blessed woman because I walk in the counsel of the Lord and not with the ungodly. I delight in the law of the Lord and meditate on it day and night. I am like a tree planted by the rivers of water that brings forth my fruit in its season. My leaf also shall not wither, and what ever I do prospers. My pregnancy will continue to blossom and

I will bring forth a healthy baby, because the Word of God cannot fail me, (Psalm1: 1-3).

The bible says the labour of the righteous leads to life. In my pregnancy and delivery I will not experience any form of death in the name of Jesus, (Proverbs 10:16).

Father, you said in your Word that because I have set my love upon you, therefore you would deliver me and set me on high. You said because I have known your name, when I call upon you, you will answer me and be with me in trouble. You also promised to deliver me and I bless you for delivering my baby for me in the name of Jesus, (Psalm 91:14-16).

I love you, O Lord my strength. You are my rock and my fortress and my deliverer. You are my shield and the horn of my salvation, you are my stronghold. I will call upon the Lord, who is worthy to be praised, so shall I be saved from my enemies, (Psalm18: 1-3).

I am delivered from the mouth of lions. The Lord has rescued me from every evil attack and will bring me safely to a blissful delivery. To him be Glory forever and ever, Amen, (2 timothy 4: 17–18).

Father I ask you to monitor my pregnancy. The bible says your eyes roam through and fro to make strong on behalf of those who fear you. Let your eyes roam through my pregnancy and make your Name strong in my life.I reject headaches, misty or blurred vision, and stomach pains, vaginal bleeding during my pregnancy. My pregnancy is ordained by God, my pregnancy is perfect. In the name Jesus I reject leakage of fluid, which suggests broken water before due date. I reject frequent painful urination during this pregnancy. I reject swollen hands, feet, and ankles, throughout my pregnancy. The Lord led His children through the wilderness and not one of them had swollen feet. I reject early morning sickness like vomiting throughout my pregnancy. I decree a blissful pregnancy into my life. I refuse to partake of the works of darkness; I am a blessed woman.

I reject any form of sickness like flu, very high temperature in the mighty name of Jesus. I decree God's grace upon my pregnancy. When my baby starts to kick his kicks will be firm and strong everyday and there will be no day I will experience less than ten kicks, from the baby in 12 hours. I reject every form of setback or sorrow in the name of Jesus.

My breast is perfect and I command it to be fully prepared to nourish my baby. The bible says my God is a heavily breasted God and He nurses me on His heavy breast. I will nurse my baby with perfect breast. I reject low-lying placenta that will prevent me from enjoying my pregnancy. I reject late delivery and I start to decree that my baby will not be early or overdue by a single day. God said I know the appointed time, father you know the appointed day of delivery for my baby and my baby will not be late by a single day. Any plague that wastes in the noonday light will not come near my pregnancy. I reject German measles and all other forms of plague during my pregnancy. The Word of God tells me in Psalm 91 that because I have made the Lord my refuge no plague shall come near my dwelling. All inherited sickness and disease will be far from this pregnancy. I am a blessed and prosperous woman. Mother of all Living.

Now make these confessions to help you over come any form of shock that can happen in pregnancy:

"From six calamities God rescues me; in seven no harm will befall me. In famine He will ransom me from death, and in battle from the stroke of the sword. I am protected from the lash of the tongue. And I need not fear when destruction comes. I will laugh at destruction and famine and need not fear the beasts of the earth. For I have a covenant with the stones of the field, and the wild animals will be at peace with me. I know that my tent is secure; and I will take stock of my property and find nothing missing. I know that my children will be many, and my descendants like the grass of the earth, (Job 5:19-25). Take glory Lord and thank you. Amen.

Blissful pregnancy and painfree childbirth faith Clinic

Every month Veronica Anusionwu and her team will hold blissful pregnancy and painfree childbirth classes. In this class we will discuss all areas of pregnancy and childbirth from the spiritual perspective. We will also invite Christian doctors and nurses to come from time to time and share with us about this topic from the medical point of view. We will then pray together and anoint you with oil to prepare you for a safe and swift delivery.

To register for one of the classes photocopy this form and return it to us now. You can call or email us for more details.

Name:

Address:

How many months pregnant are you?

Will you be interested in coming every month to our blissful pregnancy classes to arm yourself with the Word for total victory in your pregnancy and childbirth? If yes, return this form with a self addressed envelope and we will be in touch with you.

"Winning In Life Through The Anointing Oil"
By Veronica Anusionwu

"Is anyone sick? He should call the elders of the church to pray over him and anoint him with oil in the name of the Lord. And the prayer offered in faith will make the sick person well. The Lord will raise him up. If he has sinned he will be forgiven" **James 5:13-15.**

The anointing oil is one of the weapons of deliverance and victory provided for us by God. The anointing oil is a powerful tool for ministering healing to the world. While studying the bible for the writing of this book I also discovered that God uses the anointing oil as a ministry tool. The Bible says in Psalm 45:7 "Therefore God, your God, has set you above your companions by anointing you with the oil of joy." God anoints with the oil of joy, the oil of gladness, etc. This oil is spiritually applied by God to comfort us in difficult situations.

Since I discovered the anointing oil, my life has become one happy event after another. I first heard of the anointing oil through a friend who drove my cousin to Slough in London to move her luggage to a new house. On getting there she found out that her keys were not with her. She quickly moved into action. She took out her anointing oil and anointed the door, she commanded the door to open in Jesus name. She did it three times and on the third time she pushed the door and it opened. This friend confided in me that he then knew this lady was serving a living God. When I heard this, I determined to study the Bible on the subject of the anointing oil, and I asked the Holy Spirit to teach me more from His Word about this subject. As light started to come to me from God on the anointing oil, I made sure I had the anointing oil all over my home. I also got some from the church, which I mixed, in a big bottle that I bought.

The anointing oil is the safest and most powerful prescription in the world today. What is a prescription? It is the action of laying down authoritative rules or direction. A written direction or order for the preparation and use of a medicine. Medicine prescribed. It is the raw power of God in bottled oil. It is a prescription from Almighty God according to- **Ezra 7:22-23** *"—A hundred baths of olive oil...Without limit, Whatever the God of heaven has prescribed, let it be done with diligence. Here we note that God prescribed the anointing oil.* The anointing oil will penetrate through any stronghold and bring it down.

The anointing oil will heal cancer, it will heal Aids, it will heal Leukaemia, and it will heal any kind of sickness. It will restore broken homes and resurrect any dead business; it can even raise the dead. The anointing oil will deal with any deep hurt in your heart. If you feel like, emotionally, you are about to fall apart the anointing oil of His power is able to bring peace into your life. Do you have a physical affliction? Have you tried to lose weight or break your self-loose from a controlling habit? The anointing oil is able to help you. The bible tells us that the anointing will destroy the yoke. The anointing oil has no side effect; you can never use too little or too much of it. You cannot separate the anointing oil of God and the Holy Spirit. The anointing oil simply means "the power of God in bottled oil" It is a ministry tool used by the Spirit of God to destroy yokes.

The anointing oil is not a magic wand
The anointing oil is not a magic wand that you can just fling around. The anointing oil will work in all situations when used in faith in conjunction with the Word of God concerning that situation.

Testimonies about the anointing oil
My daughter had a very strange thing happening to her. Whenever we went out of the house and the air outside touched her, her body will

break out in boils and blisters. I quickly took her to the doctor and he told me she was reacting to the environment and there was nothing he could do. When I got home I opened Isaiah 53:6 where God said, "Christ has paid the price for our sickness" I anointed her with oil and received her healing for her with thanksgiving. Guess what happened. Everything stopped. The power of God and the anointing oil cannot fail. (Mrs V A London)

I started out on a ministry trip to Ghana. The night before my trip I felt led to go to Sister Veronica and ask her to anoint me with oil and commit me to God. I went to her and we spent hours praying and she anointed me with oil. I finally left her and the next day left for this trip. A few days after I arrived in Ghana I was involved in a serious car accident, where two people lost their lives. It was then that I realised the power of the anointing oil and the anointing of God. Through the strength of God I was able to survive the accident with only a scratch on my knee and was able to minister for hours to those injured in the accident before help came for us. I really encourage the use of the anointing oil for total protection of our lives. (Miss CN London)

This is taken from the book "**Winning In Life Through The Anointing Oil**" By Veronica Anusionwu. Published By The Lord's Word On Healing Publications @ **£7.00 include £1.75 for shipping**. Send your order and cheque to the address below.

Overcoming Infertility Collection

By Veronica Anusionwu

■ *Choosing Your Baby's Sex*
Here you will find all the information you need to choose the
sex of your baby. In this rich and fulfilling book, Veronica also shares
her own testimony of how she chose the sex of her own baby.

■ *Woman, You Are Not Infertile*
At last that long sought after baby. Imagine never having to think
of what you have to do in order to have a baby. It's all in here,
Just the right solution and answers you have been looking for. At
the very heart of God is an overwhelming desire to bless you with
children. All you have to do is say "Yes, God, I want to partake."
Just the right solution and answers you have been looking for.
But don't just take my word for it try it today. Before you know it
you will be hold-ing a beautiful and bouncing baby in your arms.
Yes "you " will.

■ *Man, You Are Not Infertile*
This book has it all - every information you need to overcome
in all areas of male infertility. If you want that BABY here's the solution.
This book has all the answers. "Man you are not infertile"
brings good news to those men who have been told they are infertile
and it has all the answers you need to overcome in all areas of male
infertility. It's time you discover how you can overcome male infertility and before you know it you will be cuddling your baby in your
arms.

■ *Who Said You Are Too Old To Conceive?*
This powerful book will smooth out the rough edges of the pain
and suffering you have undergone in the past. It will-

help you let go of old negative belief system.

Open you up to new ideas and approaches. Keep you looking and feeling younger, fresher and most important of all help you get what you want (a baby).

■ *Triumph Over Impotence*

At last you can triumph over impotence, achieve peak performance in your marital bed and go on to bring back the romance into your marriage. Why not? This is your time, make the most of it, go ahead and triumph over impotence.

■ *Oh! God Why All The Miscarriages?*

This fresh, new, and contemporary book gives you a fresh start. Your days of miscarriage are over. You deserve the best and this simple and easy to read book gives you all the answers you need to overcome miscarriage and go on to have live and healthy babies.

■ *Secrets To A Blissful Pregnancy And Pain Free Childbirth*

In this refreshing new book you will find everything you need for a blissful pregnancy and pain-free childbirth. Veronica Anusionwu declares the word of God; "the blessing of the Lord, it maketh rich, and he addeth no sorrow to it". God wants you to shine! He wants you to make every moment of your pregnancy special. He wants you to:

· Be spiritually, mentally and physically fit
· Be blissfully comfortable
· Be very soft. Very supple. Very sensuous. Very warm. Very sexy for your husband. Enjoy love making without pain or discomfort.

God wants you to know that delivering a child is ordained to be:

- Easy
- Pain-free.
- Without hassles
- Without problems

Brighten your day by relaxing in total comfort and get cosy with the exciting biblical confession at the back of this book. Why not? It is your time to shine in your pregnancy. Blissful pregnancy and pain-free childbirth is your heritage from the Lord.

THE LORD'S WORD ON HEALING SERIES

ORDER FORM

Yes, I want:

1)_____ Copy/copies: "Man, You Are Not Infertile" @ £10.00 each

2)_____ Copy/copies: "Woman, You Are Not Infertile" @ £10.99 each

3)_____ Copy/copies: "Choosing Your Baby's Sex" @ £2.95 each

4)_____ Copy/copies: "Oh God, Why All The Miscarriages?" @ £5.00

5)_____ Copy/copies: "Who Said You Are Too Old To Conceive?" @ £4.99

6)_____ Copy/copies: "Triumph Over Impotence" @ £5.00 each

7)_____ Copy/copies: "Winning in life Through The Anointing Oil" @ £7.00 each

8)_____Copy/copies: " Triumph Over Growths that occur in the womb " @ £6.00 each

9)_____ Copy/copies: " Secrets To A Blissful Pregnancy And Pain Free Childbirth" @ £8.00 each

Please add £1.75 postage and packing per book. Cheques or postal orders should be made payable to LWH publications.

Amount enclosed: _____

Name: _____

Address: _____

_____

_____

Mail To - LWH -PO BOX 24604 London E2 9XA

THE LORD'S WORD ON HEALING MINISTRY

FAITH CLINIC APPLICATION FORM

The purpose of the faith clinic is to help those who may need someone to stand with them in prayer and faith to receive all they need from God. The faith clinic is designed to help build faith in God and Jesus Christ for those who need it.

Answer these questions truthfully. This will help us to determine what faith class you will need to attend.

NAME: _____

AGE: _____Date:_____

ADDRESS: _____

_____

1)   How long have you been suffering from this aliment?____

2)   Have you undergone any medical check-up to diagnose the cause of sickness?

3)   What was the diagnosis? Write on a separate sheet of paper if necessary

_____

_____

_____

4)   Will you be willing to participate in a series of faith teachings from the Bible to build your faith to overcome your limitations?   **Tick**

Y E S?   **N O ?**

5)   Is there anything you want to tell us that will help in deciding what faith clinic you need to attend? (Write on a separate sheet of paper if necessary.)

YES ?   **NO ?**

Mail to:
Veronica Anusionwu, The Lords Word On Healing Ministries, PO BOX 24604, London E2 9XA

THE LORD'S WORD ON HEALING MINISTRIES

Covenant Partners Form

Dear, partner,

God has called me to bring the Healing Gospel of Jesus to the world. To accomplish this vision I am going to need Faith Covenant Partners. I have prayed that the Lord will send me faithful men and women who will stand with me both financially and spiritually to fulfil this vision. If God is laying it on your heart to partnership with me please respond now.

As a covenant partner my prayer team and I will pray for you every day, will stand with you in faith whenever you need us. In return I will expect you to sow seed monthly into this ministry or as the spirit of God leads you. Pray for my staff and me as the Spirit of God leads you.

When you sow into the work of God the Bible promises you these benefits: **Protection** (Malachi: 3 10-11). **Favour** (Luke 6:38). **Financial prosperity** (Deutronomy: 8 18).

Faith Covenant PartnerRegistration/Request Coupon

Please complete this response form and return it to me today.

Veronica, as God enables me, I will do my best to support you with a regular monthly gift.

(Standing Order Form)

To the manager: ————————————————————Bank/ building Society

Address: ————————————————————

———————————————————————— Post Code—

————————————

Please pay: LWH , Natwest Account Number: 83816976. Sort Code: 501005

Amount in Words:————————————————————

As From:(Date)————————————————————and every month/week until further notice.

My account details

The name in which my account is held: ————————————————

—Account Number: ————————---- Sort Code:————————

Signature: ——————————————————Address:—————————

Mail to:

Veronica Anusionwu

The Lords Word On Healing Ministries, PO BOX 24604, London E2 9XA. Website:WWW.Lwhpublications.org.

e-mail: info@Lwhpublications.org